W9-CUN-277

Beatrix A Siman

PRISON HOMICIDE

PRISON HOMICIDE

By

Sawyer F. Sylvester
John H. Reed
David O. Nelson

all of the

Department of Sociology and Anthropology
Bates College
Lewiston, Maine

SP Books Division of
SPECTRUM PUBLICATIONS, INC.
New York • London

Distributed by Halsted Press
A Division of John Wiley & Sons

New York   Toronto   London   Sydney

SPECTRUM PUBLICATIONS, INC.
175-20 Wexford Terrace, Jamaica, N.Y. 11432

Library of Congress Cataloging in Publication Data

Sylvester, Sawyer F
   Prison homicide.

   (Sociomedical science series)
   Bibliography: p.
   Includes index.
   1. Prison homicide–United states. 2. Prison
violence–United States. 3. Prisons and race
relations–United States. I. Reed, John H.,
1937-   joint author. II. Nelson, David O.,
joint author. III. Title.
HV9O25.S94   364.1'523'0973   77-22698
ISBN 0-89335-025-7

Contents

This book is based on the results of a study prepared under Grant #74-NI-99-0022 from the National Institute of Law Enforcement and Criminal Justice, Law Enforcement Assistance Administration, U.S. Department of Justice.

Points of view or opinions stated in this document are those of the authors and do not necessarily represent the official position or policies of the U.S. Department of Justice.

But that I am forbid
To tell the secrets of my prison-house,
I could a tale unfold whose lightest word
Would harrow up thy soul . . .

Hamlet, I, v

Acknowledgments

The authors wish to make note of the contributions to this book by other members of the original research staff. Dr. Christine Holden aided us in all areas of the research and especially in the statistical analysis. Ms. Wendy Wolfson was mainly responsible for carrying out the field survey. Finally, none of our efforts would have been successful without the devoted and long-suffering attention of our secretary, Mrs. Joan Baird of Auburn, Maine.

The jacket design is an original drawing by Lynda Litchfield Lent.

Foreword

This monograph constitutes the most comprehensive study of prison homicides yet undertaken in the United States. Data pertaining to the occurrence of homicide in male penal populations during 1973 was obtained from all states as well as federal jurisdictions. The investigation involved compilation of relevant data by local, state and federal authorities as well as extensive field work by the project staff. The end result of this eighteen-month undertaking is the present in-depth appraisal of the causes and consequences of homicides committed within prison walls.

The research findings are provocative. As expected, killings are most common among maximum security prisoners with histories of violent offenses. Unexpected, however, was the finding that gang conflicts and racial antagonism were not the predominant factors in prison homicide. With respect to mortality in prison, it was found that the crude death rate was lower than that of the non-incarcerated population, although both the suicide and homicide rates were high. Concerning the prison environment itself — staff, physical facilities, penal program — there was little evidence to support the interpretation that the occurrence of homicide is related to the presence or absence of modern rehabilitative influences.

Analysis of the detailed case histories pertaining to the 128 homicides

studied did reveal, however, that a crucial aspect of unraveling the phenomenon of prison homicide was the determination of the relationship of the
victim to his murderer. In this regard, two types of homicides were
identified: those in which there was a single assailant, and those in which
there were two or more prisoners involved as murderers. Thus, in prison, one
finds in the patterns of homicide both similarities to and differences
between those which characterize society in general. The similarities lie
in the concentration of homicides within the violence-prone segment of
the population (all of the homicides reported occurred in 27 states; 23
states had no prison homicides). The differences lie in the more instrumental
or precipitating factors — lack of fire arms, unavailability of alcohol, and
absence of family members as potential victims.

This study constitutes a major advance in our knowledge of homicide
in the United States by providing a national data base and competent
analysis of a complex social problem.

John C. Ball, Ph.D.
Temple University School
of Medicine
and
Past President,
American Society of Criminology

Preface

The practitioners of corrections share several common goals, one of which is maintaining internal order within the institution. A nucleus of internal order must be present before counseling, educational, and vocational programs can be developed. A study such as "Prison Homicide" contributes immeasurably to the establishment of that order.

The value in "Prison Homicide" lies in its effort to evaluate empirically cause and effect relationships. Administrators desperately need to understand a situation prior to initiating a knowledgeable effort to rectify the basis. Otherwise, attempts historically have used group punishment methods that further solidify inmates against staff and reinforce the inmate code of silence. Messrs. Sylvester, Reed, and Nelson have given the field a new tool with which to work, a tool that enables us to pry at the roots of the problem. Profiles have been established to such a degree of accuracy that names and faces materialize for those who have worked in corrections. It makes one wonder how many lives could have been saved had the inmates fitting these profiles and reflecting a propensity toward violence been isolated and/or programmed accordingly.

Administrators of institutions are only too aware of the impact of an unsolved murder within a compound. As in any type of community setting, unrest pervades and permeates. Behaviorists have long maintained that swift and sure punishment acts as a deterrent. Conversely, violence not punished tends to establish itself as an accepted method of accomplishing that which is desired. The ponderous machinery of our criminal justice system has raised questions concerning its efficiency and effectiveness in an open society. The problems of apathy, fear, or the inmate code of silence may keep a witness from stepping forward to solidify allegations toward an assailant in an institution. Five days in isolation for the premeditated murder of another inmate is a case documented within this script. It shocks as it should. But, it must be viewed in light of the weight given to eyewitness testimony in such matters and perceived as reality. The lack of witnesses has prevented many prosecutors from pursuing a case and has made the burden of proof an impossible task for investigators. Law enforcement officials usually feel that their most difficult cases are those which must be developed solely upon circumstantial evidence. In open society such cases are rare; in penal institutions they are the rule.

Prevention of violence has always been a high priority with prison administrators, but prevention without knowledge has proven unworkable. The wheel has been invented again and again. The sharing of knowledge gained from experience and the readaptation of internal procedures in order to benefit from that knowledge has been accepted in virtually all disciplines and certainly has great merit in institutional management.

"Prison Homicide" is a book long needed and much welcomed by those in the field of corrections.

WILLIAM E. AMOS
U.S. Board of Parole
and
President,
American Society of Criminology

Introduction

The study of homicide as it occurs in prisons would seem to be a subject of no small relevance for modern criminology and penology. In the last few years, prison unrest has been brought vividly to public notice, and part of the issue of prisoners' rights which has arisen from such unrest has been concerned with the contention that prisons have become so rife with violence as to be a continuing danger to the lives of inmates as well as staff. Moreover, the general concern with racial inequality in the United States has found its expression in penology in the contention that racial differences are a leading cause of prison violence.

Quite recently, the critical assessment of prisons which suggests that imprisonment is so damaging to human life that it should be almost totally abolished has lent support to a view of human violence as being totally caused by environmental factors to the exclusion of individual differences. This view is consistent with the general trend in American criminology over the past fifty years to approach the causes of crime almost exclusively in sociological terms.

Any study of prison violence, as such, with all the varied behavior which that term encompasses, would be an empirical task of almost incomprehensible proportions. The study of homicide in prisons is an undertaking considerably more limited in scope, but one that may—nonetheless—shed some light on the general assertions about prison violence previously mentioned. Furthermore, as a type of homicide, it may add data to those which already exist in the literature on other types of homicide.

This book is the result of a study of homicides occurring in 1973 in prisons in the United States housing adult male felons and having populations of 200 or more inmates. Included within the scope of this study are homicides which took place within or directly contiguous to penal facilities. By limiting the study to homicides in institutions for adult male felons having 200 or more inmates, several potential problems would be avoided. Some homogeneity of setting could be maintained in that reception and diagnostic centers, pre-release centers, halfway houses and local lockups were effectively excluded. In addition, these larger institutions were more easily identified, being permanent institutions of long standing. To this end, only those institutions under state and federal control were considered in the final analysis.

The calendar year 1973 was selected because it was believed that this was the most recent year for which the data would be relatively complete. Selection of a wider time interval than one year would have necessitated a compromise in the quality of the data collected on each homicide event and its participants in favor of increased quantities of data. Such a compromise was not deemed advisable.

It should be emphasized that all findings of this study are based on data taken from records routinely maintained by the criminal justice system.

An initial identification of penal facilities meeting selection criteria was obtained from a published directory of such facilities. This yielded a preliminary list of 198 institutions. As an aid in gathering information on the populations of these institutions and their homicidal behavior, a list of contacts was secured from the National Prisoner Statistics Program which named individuals in each state department of correction having responsibility for compiling prisoner statistics. A letter of introduction was forwarded to each of these contacts which introduced the project and the research instruments under preparation.

Three mailed questionnaires provided an initial view of prison homicide in 1973. A questionnaire sent to departments of correction established the number of homicides and was a major source of demographic data. Questionnaires to district attorneys and to coroners provided checks on other data. A field survey involving inspection of records of homicide events and participants, records maintained by the correctional systems, established a major general data base. Finally, through the cooperation of the Bureau of the Census, certain institutional characteristics were compared with the presence or absence of prison homicide.

Within the field survey, several research instruments were used to gather and check information on the 1973 homicides. A broad interrogatory known as the "homicide case report form" was used to gather data on homicide events and participants. Another form was used to record prison population data and some gross characteristics of prison deaths and homicides. A so-called "death sheet" was used to enumerate prison deaths in each correctional system which reported a homicide.

Two features of the research design were manifest in the development of these instruments: first, the broad exploratory nature of a national study of a phenomenon occurring intermittently in penal institutions; second, that the data available in the form of documents and records were maintained by various departments of corrections in a nonuniform manner. Consequently, the instruments were designed to maximize the data available and thus afford the adjustments which undoubtedly would have to be made to standardize such data.

The homicide case report form was carried into the field by our investigators and used to record the information they found in incident reports, inmate folders, death certificates, and psychiatric and medical records. This form contained almost exclusively open-ended questions, and was frequently altered and revised to capture a meaning which had been overlooked, to gather new data which had previously been thought unavailable, or to drop an item which apparently was not generally available in prison records.

The two-page prison survey was mailed to each state contact identified by the National Prisoner Statistics Program. In 30 states having centralized files stored in computerized archives, the forms were sent to a single contact at the department of corrections. In the 20 remaining states, the forms were sent to the appropriate institutions directly. In the final analysis, the only data elicited from these surveys were the population sizes for each institution. These population figures were used to calculate the homicide rates and other rates discussed in the findings of the study. Returns on this survey, however, were pursued in the field research and by a follow-up telephone canvass to maximize the number of facilities included in the analysis of the institutional correlates of prison homicide. Of the 198 facilities identified by the American Correctional Association directory as meeting the criteria of adult male felon institutions with a population exceeding 200, it was learned that 28 were listed erroneously due to inaccurate population figures.

The death sheet served not only as a data source, but also as a research tool utilized in the field to enumerate prison deaths leading to the identification of inmate victims. The death rates discussed in Chapter One were constructed from these data.

When a department of correction reported that its system had experienced one or more homicides during 1973, clearance to view prison records and inmate folders was requested. When this request was granted, a visit by a member of our research staff, or someone trained by our staff, was scheduled to gather data on the homicides using the homicide case report form. Upon arrival at the state department of corrections, it was usually necessary to sift through inmate death certificates for 1973 to get the names of homicide victims. In this phase of the field research operation, the death sheet was filled out. Once the list of victims' names was complete, the folders on these inmates were requested and the appropriate victim information recorded. Files of incident reports yielded data on the event and on assailants identified in the initial homicide investigation. Assailant folders were treated in similar fashion and the requisite data recorded on the open-ended forms. In the cases of staff victims, the incidents were informally recalled by members of the department and the appropriate incident and assailant folders viewed.

As the first completed homicide case report forms were returned from the field, the homicide data were standardized into closed-category variables suitable for analysis. At the outset, some 250 closed-category variables were created. Subsequent to the arrival of the first 57 prison homicide case reports, a preliminary analysis was undertaken. Those variables deemed inadequate were deleted or revised. In the final analysis, 48 variables were coded on the homicide event. Sixty-four variables considered the demographic, medical, psychological and criminal traits of the victims and assailants. Five variables coded the disposition of the assailants following the homicide. Five variables outlined the sparse data on staff victims. No data were gathered on staff assailants.

Once the coding was completed, the data were entered into a computerized master data bank where information was stored on each event and its identified participants. The actual data analysis, however, was performed using subfiles of the master data file, each of the four corresponding to the unit of analysis selected: events, inmate victims, inmate assailants and staff victims. From these data sets, complete marginal tabulations were obtained and the suggested cross-tabulations performed.

The 128 homicides considered in the analysis reflect all but one of the prison homicides found to have occurred during 1973. These homicides can be considered to be the universe of 1973 prison homicides. The advantage of this is that the values reported in this report represent the 1973 population values. Given this, and the fact that 1973 is unlikely to be representative of occurrences in other years, significance tests were deemed inappropriate.

The exhaustive procedures used at each facility to enumerate prison deaths by reviewing death certificates and the checks exercised by the district attorney and the medical examiner survey permit us to say with some confidence that all recorded 1973 prison homicides found their way into our data set. Granted, an inmate death by foul play could have been concealed by misrepresenting the death as a suicide, accident or result of natural causes; however, these instances would necessarily be among the "dark numbers of crime."

A valuable data set describing the institutional characteristics presumptively relevant to the epidemiology of prison homicide was gathered in 1974 by the Bureau of Census under the auspices of the National Prisoner Statistics Bureau's Census of State Correctional Facilities (CSCF). This data set describes 592 state correctional facilities on "type of institution," "institutional population," "employment, payroll and finances" and "facilities, services and programs." By special arrangement, it was proposed that institutional homicide rates gathered by our efforts be merged with the CSCF data to afford a comprehensive statistical perspective on the institutional correlates of prison homicide. The data set constructed at the NPS Bureau upon receipt of our data contained variables comprising three classes: variables already constructed from the CSCF to describe the aggregate characteristics of state correctional facilities and homicidal behavior; variables to be constructed by the Bureau from raw data on the CSCF; and the homicide rate based on the number of homicides divided by the total number of inmates at the facility.

One hundred and thirty facilities were included in the composite data set. Forty of the 170 adult male felon facilities with populations exceeding 200 were excluded. Twenty-eight of these were excluded because they were federal and District of Columbia facilities not considered by the CSCF. Twelve others were excluded due to insufficient information. The final data set was used in the analysis of institutional correlates of prison homicide.

The analysis of homicide events included consideration of region, time, location, method, the immediately-related milieu (including victim precipitation), racial components and institutional responses. Such analysis was structured within the general framework of a fourfold typology of inmate/inmate, inmate/staff, staff/inmate and staff/staff homicide events. These were further distinguished by the involvement of single or multiple assailants, and by time, location, method and immediately-related milieu. The characteristics of assailants and victims are presented by profiles of age, race, religion, marital status, residence, intelligence and grade achievement, criminal and prison record, military record, and occupation. Descriptions of selected prison homicides have been used for illustration.

The analysis of institutional data deals with the presence or absence of certain characteristics of institutions in relation to the presence or absence of one or more homicides in that institution in 1973. Among the characteristics considered are: size and age of institution; density of population; housing facilities; educational and racial composition of staff; existence of special facilities (educational, recreational, therapeutic, counseling, etc.); nature of prison discipline and prison privileges.

Although it is not possible adequately to summarize the findings of the study in a few sentences, a brief precis might include the following observations:

The study suggests that homicide in prison does not occur at random, nor is it ordered temporally or geographically to any significant degree. It suggests, rather, that prison homicide may be more usefully characterized by the nature of the participants—especially that of the assailants. On their records of prior violence, assailants may at least be distinguished from victims.

Among assailants, it appears that the most distinguishing features are those characterizing assailants in multiple-assailant homicides vs. those in single-assailant homicides. The former tend to be younger, urban and more intelligent. As with all assailants, they have records of prior violence, but this usually involves serious personal crimes and burglary—not homicide. They tend to be first-termers, but they are more likely to have committed a prior homicide in prison. The latter seem to have a less patterned criminal career. If not serving sentences for homicide, they are usually serving shorter sentences than assailants in multiple-assailant homicides.

When the milieu immediately related to the homicide is considered, it appears that homicides committed by multiple assailants are more rational and planned. Those of single assailants appear to be more emotional and episodic.

The study also suggests that the more general prison milieu may not be directly related to prison homicide. It suggests that certain prisons may select for those individuals with a potential for homicide. Moreover, prisons may select differentially for those who would be assailants in multiple-assailant events and for those who would be assailants in single-assailant events by providing the relevant capacitive milieu for each. In the case of single assailants, it might be homosexuality; in the case of multiple assailants, it might be the prisoner community and code, the violation of which is being punished.

Compared to many studies in criminology and penology, ours seemed to be blessed with a substantial number of data. In the pages which follow, we have chosen to present those data with as few encumbrances as possible. Our intent has been to explore prison homicide within the constraints of readily available information, anticipating that insights gained from our research would provide a point of departure for further research and theory. We do not apologize for our failure to provide a theory of prison homicide. To have attempted to substantiate a theory on the basis of these data alone would have been a dubious undertaking. In the months since the first draft of this report was completed, we have continued to reflect on the meaning of the patterns of prison homicides and hope that our readers will be stimulated to engage in similar speculation.

CHAPTER ONE

Prison Mortality

Before confronting the more closely defined topic of homicide committed by inmates in prisons, it is advisable to deal with the larger question of deaths in prisons.

The data on prison deaths are sparse and unrefined. The major source of such information is a series of Department of Justice publications which enumerates deaths for the federal and state prison systems as they are voluntarily reported on an annual basis. Statistics which are meaningful for the purposes of this report have been developed from these sources and are presented here.[1] Obviously this discussion must be limited by the shortcomings inherent in secondary data analysis techniques.

For the years 1962 to 1970, the absolute number of deaths among sentenced male felons in state and federal correctional institutions ranged between 601 in 1968 and 740 in 1962. In each of the years surveyed, the largest absolute number of deaths occurred in state prison populations, while the smallest absolute number occurred in federal prisons. The ratio of the absolute number of deaths for the two populations in any year is approximately 10 to 1. When the relative size of the state and federal populations is taken into account by the calculation of the Crude Death Rate (CDR), the ratio for this comparison is substantially reduced.[2]

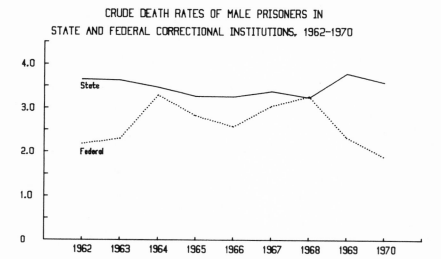

CDR = (Total Deaths / Mid-year Population) X 1000

Collectively, state prison systems tend to have proportionately higher rates of mortality than does the federal system, with the CDR for the federal system exceeding that for the states in only one year.[3]

There were 50 deaths among inmates in federal institutions for adult felons in 1966. On the basis of the mortality experience of males in the general population with the same general racial and age characteristics, 100 deaths would have been expected.[4] There were half as many deaths among males in federal prisons as would have been expected. Similarly, for 1969, where there were 44 deaths in federal penal institutions, the ratio of observed to expected deaths was .45.[5]

Using the same procedures for the 1973 population of the 27 federal institutions with over 200 male prisoners, 103 deaths would have been expected among the 18,598 men. Only 63 deaths were reported, yielding a ratio of observed to expected deaths of .61.[6]

The findings for the three years are consistent in that roughly half as many deaths as would be expected are reported each year. Further, the CDR for the federal prison system during the Sixties was only somewhat below the national average. There is little evidence to suggest that the federal prison population varied radically from those at state penal institutions. On the basis of the data from federal prisons, we would conclude that generally mortality is lower among incarcerated felons than among men in the "free world."

There are several explanations which may account for the lower general mortality rates in prison. Those prisoners suffering from degenerative diseases such as cancer or cardiovascular ailments may often be discharged from the correctional system either on parole or on unconditional release and their subsequent deaths not reported in prison bulletins. It may be that prison life, with its regimen and the restrictions it places on the lives of inmates, limits the opportunities for death by violence of all sorts, accidents, homicides and suicide. It is possible that prison life, with its adequate regular diet, rest and medical attention, simply makes inmates less susceptible to disease. Lastly, it may be that the low mortality rate is a statistical artifact resulting from the placement of dying prisoners in hospitals where their subsequent deaths are not reported as causes of inmate mortality.

The efficacy of these explanations may be probed by considering the causes of mortality among federal male felons and comparing them to the causes of mortality for a standard population of free men. We were constrained to using federal institutions because they were the only institutions for which distributions by age were available and where staff and inmate deaths were clearly separable. Data gathered for the present study on 1973 deaths in federal and selected state penal facilities divided deaths into four categories: homicide, suicide, accidents and natural causes. Rates have been calculated from these data to allow for comparisons. In addition, indirect standardization has once again been employed to determine the hypothetical mortality of the federal prison population.

First, it is useful to compare causes of mortality in large federal institutions with those in selected state institutions.[7] These distributions serve as a reminder that while the federal CDR may be lower than that for the aggregated state data, there is considerable variation in cause-specific death rates for various prisons and prison systems, and the federal system does not universally have the lowest rates. Furthermore, a word of caution is in order. The base for calculating state rates includes inmates and guards; thus these figures may be more conservative than the federal figures.

Death by natural causes in large federal prisons (23.7 deaths per thousand) falls in the top third of the distribution of death rates for natural causes for state systems whose institutions met our criteria and for which data were available. The same comparisons for accidents (.54 deaths per thousand) and suicides (4.3 deaths per thousand) for large federal institutions show that the federal institutions fall in the middle third of the respective state distributions. The homicide rate for large federal institutions (5.43 deaths per thousand) falls in the bottom third of the distribution of those institutions for which we have data. It must be kept in mind that, with the exception of homicide rates, the data on which these distributions are based were available only for those systems which had homicides. Thus the distributions are unlikely to be representative of all states.

If the absolute frequencies of observed and expected causes of death are compared for federal institutions, it can be seen that deaths from natural causes are six-tenths as likely as would be expected. Deaths from accidents are about one-twentieth as likely as would be expected in the general population. However, deaths by suicide are twice as likely, while the expected and observed number of deaths by homicide are identical. Comparatively, accidental deaths rarely occur in prisons because of the low levels of exposure to the most frequent causes of accidents—motor vehicles, conflagrations and drowning—occurring outside prison.[8]

The picture becomes clearer if the relative frequencies for the observed and expected numbers of death for each cause are compared. The proportion of deaths by natural causes is almost the same for the observed and expected distributions. The percentage for accidents is substantially lower for the observed distribution (2%) than for the expected distribution (18%), while the percentages of deaths by suicide and homicide for the observed distribution (13% and 16%, respectively) is substantially higher than for the expected distribution (4% and 9%, respectively).

Thus it appears that prison environment is healthier and at the same time more free of accidents. On the other hand, prison life may be conducive to acts of self-destruction and to acts that are destructive to the lives of others.

Several words of caution are in order concerning the expected numbers of homicides. The expectancies for dying by homicide are based on the experience of all males. The general rates reflect differential propensities for homicide victimization that are not necessarily present in the penal milieu. For instance, the age-specific homicide victimization rate for non-white men between the ages of 18 and 25 is roughly 13 per thousand. The rate for white men in the same age cohort is 1 per thousand. This difference in victimization rate may be due to differences in the predominant life styles of the two racial groups which may be ameliorated in prison.

In the federal system in 1973, there were essentially equal probabilities of homicide victimization for whites and other racial groups. Sixty-six percent of the federal inmates were of the white race. Six of the homicide victims were white. Three of the victims were black. One was an American Indian. Race does not have the impact on federal prison homicide victimization rates that it does on "free world" homicide victimization rates.

It seems reasonable to assume that deviants from the norms prohibiting violence comprise a larger proportion of the male prison population than the general male population in America. This suggests that more homicides would occur in the federal prison system than would be expected, based on the standard population figures drawn from the pool of all American males. Given this greater propensity for homicidal violence as evidenced by the lack of a racial difference in homicide victimization rates, one might have expected that more homicides would have occurred in the federal system than were actually reported. One might suggest that some effective control in limiting the level of homicidal violence in federal prisons is exercised. This is not to say, however, that this control is optimal in that homicides still occur at a rate comparable to the national average in institutions where control is one of the primary functions.

Notwithstanding the preceding discussion of mortality and homicide victimization in federal prisons, homicide is an important problem in a number of state correctional systems. The national inmate homicide victimization rate was 7.44 per ten thousand inmates compared with the federal inmate homicide victimization rate of 5.43 deaths per ten thousand inmates. The federal rate was exceeded by the inmate homicide victimization rate in 21 states and the District of Columbia. Twenty-nine states had lower inmate homicide victimization rates in their large facilities for adult male felons than did the federal system. This latter group includes 23 states which reported no inmate homicide deaths in their large male felon facilities during 1973.

According to the 1973 census of state correctional facilities, there were 42,083 full-time payroll staff at those state facilities housing more than 200 adult male felons. Eleven staff homicide deaths were reported, yielding a staff victimization rate of 2.62 per ten thousand staff members. At face value, it would appear that staff members are approximately one-third as likely as inmates to be victims of homicide. However, the payroll staff figures used in calculating this rate do not perfectly convey the "population-at-risk." These staff figures include, for example, small but significant numbers of administrative personnel who do not run the same risk of homicide victimization as custodial personnel.

Regardless of the precision of this statistic, when it is projected over 20 years of service at a penal facility it defines a real occupational hazard. In that period, a staff member faces the possibility of being the 1 in 200 staff members who will be slain in the line of duty. However, it should be noted that when the reported inmate homicide victimization rate is projected over a 20-year sentence the inmate facing that mandatory sentence has 1 chance in 67 of being a homicide victim before completing his term.

Table I
Crude Death Rates of Male Felons
In State and Federal Correctional Institutions, 1962–1970[a]

	1962	1963	1964	1965	1966	1967	1968	1969[b]	1970[b]	Total
State										
Midyear population[c]	188,824	187,565	186,536	184,468	178,586	171,912	166,398	166,786	170,986	
Total deaths	690	681	647	602	580	582	539	631	612	
Crude death rate	3.65	3.63	3.47	3.26	3.25	3.39	3.24	3.78	3.58	3.47
Federal										
Midyear population[c]	22,910	22,614	21,548	20,572	19,430	18,770	18,985	18,971	19,117	
Total deaths	50	52	71	58	50	57	62	44	36	
Crude death rate	2.18	2.30	3.29	2.82	2.57	3.04	3.27	2.32	1.88	2.63
Total										
Midyear population[c]	211,734	210,179	208,084	205,040	198,016	190,682	185,383	185,757	190,103	
Total deaths	740	733	718	660	630	639	601	675	648	
Crude death rate	3.50	3.49	3.45	3.22	3.18	3.35	3.24	3.63	3.41	3.39

[a]From the National Prisoner Statistics series, *Prisoners in State and Federal Institutions for Adult Felons*, Washington. 1962-1972.
[b]Internal consistency of population figures for these years is suspect.
[c]Average of population January 1 and December 31.

Table II

Numbers and Relative Frequencies of Observed and Expected Deaths in Federal Prisons in 1973 by Cause of Death

Cause of Death	Observed Number	Deaths Relative Frequency of Observed Number	Expected Number	Relative Frequency of Expected Number	Ratio of Observed to Expected
Natural	44	70%	73	70%	.60
Accident	1	2%	18	17%	.06
Suicide	8	13%	4	4%	2.00
Homicide	10	16%	10	10%	1.00
Total	63	101%	105[a]	101%	

[a]This value is discrepant from the 103 expected deaths given elsewhere in this report. The discrepancy is due in part to a rounding error which is compounded when calculations are made on four distributions rather than one, as is the case here. It may also be that there is a reporting error in the *Vital Statistics* volume from which age-specific death rates by cause were taken.

Table III

Populations, Deaths and Crude Death Rates in State Correctional Systems, 1962-1970[a]

States Ordered by Crude Death Rate	Population 1/1/62	Population 12/31/70	Deaths	Crude Death Rate (Per 1,000)[b]
West Virginia	2,207	938	81	6.119
Mississippi	2,068	1,730	96	5.642
Arkansas[c]	2,076	1,651	64	5.444
Alabama	5,540	3,790	218	5.435
Kansas	2,627	1,902	111	4.923
Kentucky	3,703	2,849	135	4.914
Montana[c]	648	521	17	4.416
Georgia	6,851	5,113	242	4.311
Massachusetts	1,978	2,053	72	4.126
Louisiana	3,828	4,196	147	4.079
Illinois	9,611	6,381	292	4.069
Washington	2,401	2,864	98	3.939
Wyoming[d]	425	231	11	3.932
Oregon	1,799	1,800	66	3.869
Oklahoma	2,693	3,640	100	3.860
Tennessee	3,144	3,268	108	3.841
Iowa	2,418	1,747	69	3.746
Missouri	3,930	3,413	119	3.743
Colorado	2,147	2,066	81	3.684
Utah	638	491	21	3.678
Arizona	1,592	1,461	53	3.561
Virginia	5,734	4,648	148	3.539
South Carolina	2,144	2,769	74	3.501
Florida	7,615	9,187	235	3.498
New York	17,569	12,059	489	3.478
Ohio	11,155	9,185	336	3.452
Pennsylvania	8,047	6,289	200	3.276
New Hampshire	191	244	6	3.225
Hawaii	583	256	12	3.195
California	23,927	25,033	745	3.122
North Dakota[c]	228	182	4	3.026
Michigan	9,197	9,074	214	3.012
Idaho	552	411	12	2.992
Indiana	5,372	4,137	118	2.946
Minnesota[c]	2,016	1,652	31	2.901
Texas	11,890	14,331	322	2.838
Maryland[c]	5,745	5,083	88	2.730

Table III (Continued)

States Ordered by Crude Death Rate	Population 1/1/62	Population 12/31/70	Deaths	Crude Death Rate (Per 1,000)[b]
Maine	766	516	16	2.729
Nebraska	1,328	1,000	27	2.634
Federal	22,806	19,321	480	2.624
Connecticut	1,639	1,630	36	2.480
South Dakota[c]	571	489	8	2.438
Nevada	431	689	12	2.354
Wisconsin	2,953	2,973	57	2.318
New Mexico	1,243	742	16	1.789
New Jersey	4,572	5,704	73	1.669
Vermont	319	162	3	1.335
District of Columbia[c]	2,132	1,268	12	1.162
Rhode Island[c]	262	350	1	0.568

[a]Data for some states are based on the years 1962-1967. Alaska, Delaware and North Carolina are excluded. All male and female deaths are included, except executions. (From the National Prisoner Statistics Series, *Prisoners in State and Federal Institutions for Adult Felons;* and *Executions.* Washington, 1963-1972.

[b]The crude death is based on the number of person-years lived, calculated from the mid-year population which was the average of the population on January 1, and December 31 for each year. The population figures presented in columns 2 and 3 give some indications of population trends for each state.

[c]Data for these states are based on the years 1962-1967.

[d]Includes only Wyoming State Penitentiary after 1963.

Table IV Death Rates in State Prisons in 1973

Natural Causes		Accidental		Suicide		Homicide	
Oklahoma	37.43	Nebraska	16.08	Rhode Island	26.99	Hawaii	48.90
Indiana	31.88	Rhode Island	13.50	Kansas	22.65	Virginia	34.70
Tennessee	30.22	Arizona	11.18	Hawaii	17.67	Louisiana	30.73
Texas	29.76	Kentucky	6.74	Oklahoma	9.36	Massachusetts	30.43
Georgia	23.40	Washington	6.13	Indiana	8.70	District of Columbia	29.41
Nevada	22.90	Kansas	5.66	Nebraska	8.04	Kentucky	28.97
Arizona	22.37	Colorado	3.84	Washington	6.13	Nevada	27.83
Washington	21.47	Indiana	2.90	Arizona	5.60	Rhode Island	22.68
Pennsylvania	20.59	Tennessee	2.52	Tennessee	5.04	Nebraska	21.03
Virginia	20.10	Florida	2.26	Louisiana	4.31	Missouri	20.81
Kentucky	16.86	Louisiana	2.16	Colorado	3.84	Oklahoma	20.58
Louisiana	15.09	New Jersey	2.13	Kentucky	3.37	West Virginia	19.66
Missouri	13.66	Ohio	1.02	Pennsylvania	2.74	Utah	19.05
West Virginia	13.41	Texas	.66	Missouri	2.73	Alabama	18.92
Alabama	13.22	Alabama	0	Texas	2.64	Washington	12.74
Iowa	12.08	Georgia	0	Michigan	2.62	California	11.29
Michigan	11.79	Hawaii	0	Ohio	1.02	Florida	8.53
Colorado	11.52	Iowa	0	Alabama	0	Kansas	8.30
Kansas	11.32	Michigan	0	Florida	0	Indiana	7.54
Florida	10.17	Missouri	0	Georgia	0	Nation	7.44
Nebraska	8.04	Nevada	0	Iowa	0	Tennessee	6.67
New Jersey	6.41	Oklahoma	0	Nevada	0	Georgia	5.51
Ohio	4.09	Pennsylvania	0	New Jersey	0	Ohio	5.49
Hawaii	0	Utah	0	Virginia	0	Federal	5.43
Rhode Island	0	Virginia	0	West Virginia	0	Colorado	5.13
Utah	0	West Virginia	0			Michigan	3.44
						New Jersey	2.94
						Illinois	2.10
						Pennsylvania	1.97
						Texas	.75

The rate is expressed in terms of deaths per ten thousand inmates and staff.

This table includes only inmates and staff at adult male felon facilities with an inmate population exceeding 200, and which had a homicide.

Death rates for natural causes, accidents and suicides could not be computed for the federal, District of Columbia and Massachusetts systems due to the unavailability of data on staff population. For California, the death information was for inmates only and was thus excluded.

CHAPTER TWO

Characteristics of Homicide Events

Homicide events in prison can be classified by the statuses of the participants. If it is assumed that there are two statuses, staff and inmate, for victims and for assailants in prison homicide events, a fourfold table can be constructed to represent the possible relations of the victim and his assailant.[1] If, as an additional condition, we concern ourselves with the cases in which no assailants were identified, the result is a sixfold typology.

In our sample of 128 homicides in 1973, there were 78 inmate/inmate homicide events. In addition, there were 10 inmate/staff events, 3 staff/inmate events and 1 staff/staff event. There were 35 instances which have been classified as unidentified assailant/inmate events and 1 unidentified assailant/staff event.

In the main, the remainder of this report will be concerned with the inmate/inmate and inmate/staff events. In part, this decision was necessitated by the small number of events in three of the four remaining types. In a subsequent section, unidentified assailant/inmate events will be discussed briefly.

Before proceeding, the two principal types of events should be compared in terms of whether they were single- or multiple-assailant events. Assailants appear to have acted alone in 63% of the inmate/inmate events.

Guards are more likely to have been attacked and killed by groups than by individuals. Finally, it should be pointed out that there were 128 identified assailants for the 78 inmate/inmate homicides. This should be kept in mind when the characteristics for the assailants in inmate/inmate events are discussed. Unfortunately, the number of assailants for this type of event and the total number of events are identical: they should not be confused. There were 24 identified assailants in the 11 inmate/staff homicides; one group of 4 was responsible for 2 staff deaths.

LOCATION AND TIME

During 1973, homicides occurred at 54 of the 170 institutions which met the criteria for inclusion in our universe of prisons. These facilities were under the jurisdiction of 29 states, the District of Columbia and the federal system. The South had the largest absolute number of homicides (56), followed by the West (32), the North Central region (18) and the Northeast and federal system (11 apiece).[2] When the regions and the federal system are ranked by the number of deaths per ten thousand inmate population, the Western region leads the nation, followed by the South, the North Central region, the federal system and the Northeast. The risk of a homicide to an inmate in the West and South was at least one and a half times as great as it was in the rest of the country.

Temporally, prison homicides in 1973 were fairly evenly distributed over the months of the year. There were more homicides in August, May and November than would be expected if homicides occurred by chance, while there were fewer than would be expected in the months of April and October. Inmate/staff homicides were most likely to occur during the summer months.

The probability of a prison homicide occurring on a Thursday or a Sunday was about .2 for either day. Friday was the only day of the week when the probability of a homicide was about the same as would be expected if homicidal assaults were evenly distributed. There were proportionately fewer homicides on the remaining days of the week.

Prison homicides occurred more frequently in the afternoon than at any other time of the day. Slightly more than 50% of all homicides took place in the afternoon and the early evening. The periods of greatest risk were Thursday and Saturday afternoons, respectively. There were almost no differences by type of homicide.

One-quarter of all prison homicides occurred in a participant's cell, and in all cases but one this was the cell of the victim. The one case where the homicide took place in the assailant's cell involved self-defense. An addi-

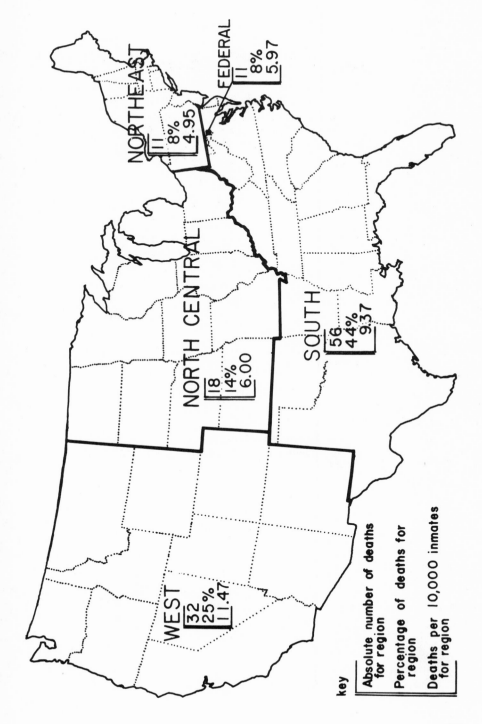

NORTHEAST
11
8%
4.95

FEDERAL
11
8%
5.97

NORTH CENTRAL
18
14%
6.00

SOUTH
56
44%
9.37

WEST
32
25%
11.47

key

Absolute number of deaths for region

Percentage of deaths for region

Deaths per 10,000 inmates for region

tional third of the homicides occurred in the cell block or in the dormitory. Outside of the living quarters, homicides were most likely to occur in recreation areas such as television rooms, gymnasiums, inmate coffee shops or the library. About 10% of all homicides occurred in exposed areas within the prison, such as yards. Although most common in living areas, homicides did occur in every conceivable location in the institution, with the notable exception of visiting areas and infirmaries.

METHODS

Stabbing was the most common method of inflicting death. This reflects the fact that stabbing weapons are probably the most lethal weapons which are readily available to prisoners. Three-quarters of all victims died by stabbing. Ten victims (about 8%) were strangled. About 5% of the victims were beaten to death with bludgeons or personal weapons, while an equal number were killed by firearms.[3] In 5 cases, inmate assailants took advantage of the restrictive nature of prison cells to destroy victims by arson. In each case, inflammable fluids were poured into the victim's cell and ignited.

INTERVAL BETWEEN ASSAULT AND DEATH

Perhaps the most salient feature of these prison homicides is the extreme violence and brutality associated with them. The victims were often battered and beaten, but more often were stabbed to an extent which seemed to exceed that necessary to inflict death.[4] One index of the brutality might be the elapsed time between the assault and the time the victim was pronounced dead. For those cases where this information was available, half the victims were found to be dead within the same hour of the day as the assault; an additional 20% were found dead in the next subsequent hour of the day. Only 3 victims lived longer than a week, with 1 surviving 20 days.

THE IMMEDIATELY RELATED MILIEU

On the homicide case report forms, there was an open-ended question asking for "motive." Once the data were in hand, the responses to this question were reviewed, and nine categories were developed which best seemed to summarize the data on the circumstances immediately surrounding the homicide.[5] Recognizing that motive is in all likelihood a multidimensional phenomenon, primary, secondary and tertiary motives were coded in accordance with their prominence in the accounts of the event.

No motive could be ascertained from the data in nearly a quarter of the cases. In 15 of the events homosexuality was a primary motive, and in 6 additional events it was a secondary motive, making it the most common motivational factor in prison homicides. "Snitching"—informing on others—was involved in 16 cases. Arguments resulted in 15 homicides, while quarrels over money and property seem to have precipitated another 14. Twelve homicides were attendant to larger melees and were coded as fights. Quarrels related to drugs and intoxicants resulted in 11 deaths. Gang activity and racial tension were involved in 9 and 7 killings, respectively.

Each homicide event was judged on whether the victim might have precipitated his own death. About 20% of the homicides appeared to have been victim-precipitated. Of these 24 slayings, 5 were clearly cases of self-defense on the part of the assailant, 3 were justifiable homicide by guards, and 16 were cases where the victim generally provoked the incident which led to his own demise. No guards were identified as having precipitated their deaths.

RACIAL COMPONENTS

Of the 112 inmate victims for which race was known, 56% were white.[6] This percentage is very close to the median percentage (54%) of whites in large state-run institutions for adult male felons for which information was available. Sixty-six percent of the inmates of the federal system are of the white race.

Six of the 10 homicide victims in the federal system were white. It can tentatively be concluded that victimization occurs in rough proportion to the racial composition of prison populations. However, the pattern of homicide victimization in prisons is at variance with that of the general population of adult males. For instance, the age-specific homicide victimization rate for non-white men between the ages of 18 and 25 is roughly 13 per thousand. The rate for white men in the same age cohort is 1 per thousand. It is possible that an explanation for this lies in the fact that the sociocultural factors which create the discrepancies in the homicide victimization rates of the two racial moieties in the general population are ameliorated by the conditions of prison life.

Ten of the 11 guard victims of inmates were white. The median percentage of white custodial personnel in state prisons is slightly more than 93%. Thus white and non-white custodial personnel are slain at rates comparable to their respective proportions in the population-at-risk.

The same pattern of correspondence between aggregate racial character- istics and the racial make-up of the population holds for assailants, al- though some caution needs to be exercised since there was a fairly large number of events where assailants remained unidentified.[7] Fifty-eight per cent of the identified assailants were of the white race, which is very close to the percentage of white in state and federal institutions—54% and 63%, respectively.

When race is considered in conjunction with some of the other charac- teristics which differentiate various types of prison homicide, the propor- tion of white and non-white inmates does not vary greatly from the medi- ans of the populations. Fifty-one percent of the inmate assailants who acted alone were white, while 61% of the inmate assailants who acted in concert with other assailants were white. On this basis, it can be concluded that there are no salient characteristics on which victims and assailants of one race were disproportionately represented in comparison with their numbers in the total population.

We now turn to the matter of whether prison homicide events are dis- proportionately interracial. Using 58% as the figure for the proportion of white inmates in the prison population and 42% for the proportion of blacks, the proportion of inmate/inmate events which could reasonably be expected to be interracial may be determined. Making the multiple as- sumptions that events are independent, that the race of the participants is independent, and that there is a single victim and a single assailant, roughly 48% of the homicide events could be expected to involve participants of different races. Assuming that 93% of the guards are white, the expecta- tion of an interracial event in the case of a guard victim is 43%.

A comparison of these expectations with the actual data can be ac- complished in two ways. The first method involves checking the circum- stances of the homicide events as reported in institutional records to see what percentage involved racial motives. The data suggest that 4% of the events in which an inmate was a victim were racially motivated, while 8% of the events in which a guard was a victim had racial overtones. No more than 5% of all events seemed to involve racial antagonisms; moreover, if all of the events in which motives were unknown were to have been racially inspired, the total could still be no higher than 31%. Either way, the percentage of interracial events is dramatically different from the ex- pected values in the mid-forties.

A second way to judge the interracial character of events is to compare the races of the victims and assailants. The data show that 11% of the white victims were slain by a non-white assailant or group of assailants, while 14% of the non-white victims were slain by a white assailant or group of white assailants. If it turned out that all of the inmate/inmate events in which assailants were unidentified had assailants whose race was different from that of the victim, the proportion of interracial homicides would begin to approximate the expected number. Even so, the number of interracial events would still be smaller than expected. Furthermore, there is very little reason to believe that any sizable proportion of the events in which assailants were unidentified would turn out to be interracial. Indeed, one could make the argument that assailants in interracial events might be more likely to be identified by prison authorities and by members of the race of the victim.

Five of the 11 (45%) inmate/guard events involved assailants or victims of different races. This is almost identical to the expected number, although some caution should be exercised in interpretation because of the low number of events.

Using the second criterion, 19 homicides could be labeled interracial. Seven of these were cases where a white inmate or inmates killed a black inmate; 7 were cases where a black inmate or inmates killed a white inmate. Four cases involved a non-white assailant or assailants who killed a white guard, and 1 was a case where a group of whites killed a black guard. These 19 assaults occurred in 16 prisons. Only 2 prisons had more than one interracial homicidal assault. One of these—a prison which has figured prominently in discussions of the racial component of prison homicide in the news—had 3 interracial events. The second prison had 2 interracial events.

The question arises whether prisons in which interracial homicides occur are different from those which have intraracial homicides. It was possible to compare the two groups of prisons on five characteristics: percentage of the population under 24 years of age, percentage of the population which was white, percentage of the population consisting of personal offenders, percentage of the population serving life sentences or death sentences, and the homicide rate. The comparison is only of institutions which had a homicide in 1973, and some caution needs to be exercised because of the amount of missing data. However, it is clear that there is no substantial difference on any of the five population characteristics.

Previously, it was shown that—in the aggregate—non-whites are no more likely to be the victims of prison homicide than whites. Beyond this, it can be asked whether the racial composition of the prisoner population or the racial composition of the custodial staff is related to the incidence of prison homicide. There appears to be a low negative association between the percentage of non-white prisoners and the homicide status of the institution. There is a low positive association between the percentage of non-white custodial personnel and the homicide status of the institution, and between the racial composition of the custodial staff and the racial composition of the inmate population.

When the racial composition of the custodial staff is introduced as a control between the racial composition of the inmate populations and homicide status, the magnitude of the relationship between racial composition of the inmate population and homicide status changes very slightly, but the sign of the correlation remains the same. The interaction between race of the custodial staff and race of the inmates does not affect the original relationship between racial composition of the inmates and the homicide status of the institution.

RACE AND INSTITUTIONAL RESPONSE

If the focus of the analysis is shifted from events to assailants, the validity of some of the claims of minority groups about discrimination in the penal and criminal justice systems can be evaluated. In the case of prison homicide, white and non-white assailants are identified in proportion to their numerical strength in the population. However, when we consider what happens to assailants once they have been identified, race becomes a factor. Black assailants are 8% more likely to receive some type of prison discipline than whites. Persons of Spanish origins (15 of the 16 inmates in the "other" category) are 13% more likely than whites to have received some form of prison discipline. Blacks are 12% more likely than whites to be referred to a prosecutor and 18% more likely to be indicted for murder or some lesser charge. Assailants of Spanish origin are least likely to be referred for prosecution and indictment.

The most interesting finding is that once blacks and whites reach the courts they have almost equal probabilities of being convicted. None of the inmates in the "other" category were convicted. The percentage differences between blacks and whites are not large, given the relatively small numbers involved, although, for indictments, a minimum of 11 cases would have to change in order for the percentages to be similar. The important point is that some objective differences exist which would lend credence to inmates' subjective feelings about the differential treatment of the various racial groups within the penal milieu.

GENERAL PATTERNS OF INSTITUTIONAL RESPONSE

Institutions differentially used the resources of the criminal justice system to investigate prison deaths. It has already been shown that race of the assailant conditions the institutional response. The pattern of institutional response to a violent death varies widely in relation to other characteristics of the events and the participants.[8]

Of the total 128 cases, we have positive knowledge that the coroner was consulted 108 times and not consulted in an additional 5 cases. Thus the coroner was the one legal agent who was most often known to have conducted an inquiry. Coroners were less apt to have been consulted in cases of guard deaths than in inmate deaths.

In 78 cases, the medical cause of death appeared on the victim's death certificate.[9] Forty-five died of exsanguination. Eleven died from shock. Ten were asphyxiated. Eight were known to have perished from head injuries. Three died of burns.

Autopsies were known to have been performed on 73% of all victims. There were 13 cases where it was known that post-mortem examinations or autopsies had not been performed. In 16% of all cases, no information whatsoever was available concerning autopsies. Where information was known about the presence or absence of post-mortem examinations, there was little difference between cases of inmate victims and cases of guard victims.

Available autopsy reports yielded little information on the physical state of the victim prior to his death. Among those cases where the report was available, there was evidence in 1 case that the inmate victim was under the influence of narcotics. In 3 cases, alcohol was discovered in the inmate's corpse. Nothing unusual was reported in guard autopsies.

In 89 cases, it was known that the public prosecutor had a hand in the disposition of the homicide, while in 25 cases this office was not involved. Homicides were referred to the state police more than any other investigative police agency. Sheriffs' offices were consulted the next most often. Local police departments were consulted least often. The Federal Bureau of Investigation conducted investigations of most federal homicides and most of those occurring at the District of Columbia's penal facilities.

Characteristically, prison homicides are referred to a single police investigative agency. In only 2 cases was more than one police force involved in a homicide investigation.[10] Moreover, in 23 cases, or 20% of the homicides, prison officials investigated the event without outside police assistance.

Five different types of prison homicide investigations can be identified—four corresponding to each of the different police agencies called into the institution and one for those cases where it was known that no police agency was called. These five different investigative modes display widely varying rates of efficiency with respect to identifying suspected assailants and developing sufficient evidence to lead to one or more indictments and convictions.

State police agencies showed the highest rates of clearance, identifying one or more assailants in 81% of all cases to which they were referred. Indictments were returned in 68% of these cases, leading to convictions in 17 cases. Local police departments were called into only 4 cases but were able to identify assailants in 3 of them. Sheriffs' offices were called into more cases than the local police but had more modest rates of success. The FBI, which had sole jurisdiction in the federal system and District of Columbia, seemed to have less success than other investigative agencies in homicide clearances. They identified assailants in fewer than half the cases, and their investigations led to only one conviction. In those cases where the prison authorities handled the investigation themselves, assailants were often identified. Indictments, however, were less frequently returned against the assailants. Among those indicted, fewer than one-half were convicted.

The effective areas of institutional response to homicides varied with the status of victim, but the disposition of the assailants by the criminal justice system did not. One or more suspected assailants were identified in 91% of all cases where the victims were guards. On the other hand, suspects were identified in 69% of all cases where prisoners were the victims. Seventy-three percent of all guard homicides led to indictments. Forty-eight percent of inmate homicides resulted in formal charges. However, the courts returned convictions in 27% of guard homicides and 26% of all cases where the victims were inmates.

Among the 8 cases of staff homicides resulting in an indictment, 7 involved indictments for murder. One led to an indictment for a lesser crime. Three of these cases were known to have ended in a conviction: 2 for murder, one for a lesser crime. Of the 54 cases of inmate homicide yielding indictments, 48 were cases of indictment for murder. The remaining 6 cases led to indictments for lesser offenses. Of the 30 cases with convictions for killing an inmate, 25 were for murder and 5 were for lesser offenses.

ACTION TAKEN ON ASSAILANTS

In 4 of the 128 cases of prison homicide in 1973, the assailants were guards and therefore were not treated in the same manner as the inmate assailants. In 36 cases, the assailants were not identified; however, the information on believed number of assailants yielded the figure of 20 cases in which there were unknown single or multiple assailants.

In the remaining 88 cases, 152 assailants were identified. A study of the varying combinations and increasing degrees of punishment possible within the correctional and judicial systems yields the following observations:

For 17 of the assailants (11%), no known movement took place; only 1 assailant was paroled. Eighty-seven (57%) received a new custody designation, but since almost three-quarters of the assailants were already in maximum-security units, this was frequently a transfer to segregation. Nineteen assailants (13%) were eventually transferred to another penal institution; 3 were transferred to nonpenal institutions.

Thirty assailants (20%) received only disciplinary action within the prison system; 20 (13%) were involved only with the courts. The majority—88 (58%)—received both prison and outside discipline.

One hundred five (69%) of the 152 assailants were indicted on murder or other charges; 38 (25%) were not indicted, and the disposition of 9 (6%) is unknown. Of those indicted, prosecution was dropped against 19 assailants (13%), and in 9 cases (6%) the prosecution was pending as of the date of completion of the field research. The exact status of 24 (16%) could not be determined. However, prosecutions resulting in convictions on charges of murder, manslaughter and conspiracy were returned for 47 assailants (31%). Seventeen (11%) were found not guilty, 3 of them by reason of insanity.

This finding shows that of those indicted whose cases were completed by the courts, there was a conviction rate of 45%, a rate which might conceivably be higher if we could determine the pending and unknown categories. Since the conviction rate reported by district attorneys is considerably higher, it seems probable that prison folders on assailants are a less reliable source for disposition information.

However, if one divides the assailants into those who killed guards and those who killed inmates, some striking differences emerge.

There were 24 assailants identified as guard-killers and 128 identified as inmate-killers. Of that number, 75% of the guard-assailants had both prison and outside action, and only 55% of the inmate-assailants had both. Thirteen percent of both the guard-assailants and inmate-assailants were dealt with only in the judicial process; 4% of the guard-assailants and 23% of the inmate-assailants received only prison action. In 8% of the guard-assailant cases and 9% of the inmate-assailant cases, no known action was taken. If one disregards the cases in which no known action took place, it is clear that a much greater number of guard-assailants—87% vs. 68%—were involved with the judicial process. In cases where an inmate could reasonably be identified as connected to a guard-killing, it appears that strong efforts were made to ensure prosecution.

However, the ratios of those who were dealt with judicially and then

INMATE   ASSAILANTS — <u>TOTAL</u>

152 ASSAILANTS IDENTIFIED	88 RECEIVED PRISON ACTION & REFERRED TO THE JUDICIAL PROCESS	105 INDICTED	47 FOUND GUILTY
			17 FOUND NOT GUILTY
			7 PROSECUTION PENDING
	20 REFERRED TO THE JUDICIAL PROCESS ALONE		19 PROSECUTION DROPPED
	30 PRISON ACTION ALONE		
	14 NO ACTION OR ACTION UNKNOWN	3 NOT INDICTED	15 PROSECUTION STATUS UNKNOWN

indicted are quite comparable for the inmate-assailants and guard-assailants: 68% of the former were dealt with judicially, and 66% were indicted; all 87% of the latter were indicted.

The prosecution data seem to indicate that the cases made for the guard-assailants were much weaker, since only 4 of the 21 indicted (19%)

INMATE ASSAILANTS OF INMATE VICTIMS

128 ASSAILANTS IDENTIFIED	70 RECEIVED PRISON ACTION & REFERRED TO THE JUDICIAL PROCESS	84 INDICTED	43 FOUND GUILTY
	17 REFERRED TO THE JUDICIAL PROCESS ALONE		11 FOUND NOT GUILTY
			5 PROSECUTION PENDING
	29 PRISON ACTION ALONE		16 PROSECUTION DROPPED
			9 PROSECUTION STATUS UNKNOWN
	12 NO ACTION OR ACTION UNKNOWN	3 NOT INDICTED	

were found guilty, and in 9 cases (43%) the result was either the dropping of the case or a verdict of not guilty. Even if one assumed that half of the cases pending would be decided as guilty, and also added in half the cases of unknown disposition, the conviction rate would be considerably below that for the inmate-assailants.

INMATE ASSAILANTS OF GUARD VICTIMS

24 ASSAILANTS IDENTIFIED	18 RECEIVED PRISON ACTION & REFERRED TO THE JUDICIAL PROCESS	21 INDICTED	4 FOUND GUILTY
			6 FOUND NOT GUILTY
			2 PROSECUTION PENDING
			3 PROSECUTION DROPPED
	3 REFERRED TO THE JUDICIAL PROCESS ALONE		6 PROSECUTION STATUS UNKNOWN
	1 PRISON ACTION ALONE		
	2 NO ACTION OR ACTION UNKNOWN		

Of the 84 inmate-assailants indicted, 43 (51%) were found guilty; in 32% of the cases, either there was a verdict of not guilty or the prosecution was dropped. In 5 cases, prosecution was still pending.

One can therefore tentatively suggest that anyone involved in a guard-killing is likely to be prosecuted; such an individual is not as likely to be convicted.

Table I

Month and Relative Frequency of Homicide

January	7%
February	7%
March	8%
April	5%
May	11%
June	9%
July	8%
August	12%
September	9%
October	6%
November	10%
December	8%
Total	100%
	(128)

The expectation for any month is approximately 8%.

Table II

Day of Homicide by Time Period

Day	Midnight–6 A.M.	6 A.M.–Noon	Noon–6 P.M.	6 P.M. – Midnight	Unknown	Percentage
Sunday	.8%	4.7%	3.9%	5.5%	3.9%	18.8%
Monday	0%	2.3%	5.5%	1.6%	3.1%	12.5%
Tuesday	2.3%	1.6%	3.1%	1.6%	2.3%	10.9%
Wednesday	2.3%	1.6%	1.6%	5.5%	.8%	11.8%
Thursday	0%	3.9%	9.4%	2.3%	3.9%	19.5%
Friday	1.6%	1.6%	3.1%	3.1%	4.7%	14.1%
Saturday	1.6%	3.1%	7.0%	.8%	0%	12.5%
Percentage by time period	8.6%	18.8%	33.6%	20.4%	18.7%	100.1%

Table III
Location of Homicide
by Victim Status

Location	Inmate	Guard	Total
Cell of participant	28%		25%
Cell block or dormitory	30%	67%	34%
Hallway	3%	8%	4%
Recreation areas			
(Coffee shops, gyms, libraries)	8%	8%	9%
Dining areas	3%		3%
Kitchen	3%	8%	3%
Training areas			
(shops, classrooms)	4%		4%
Yards	9%	8%	9%
Administrative offices	2%		2%
Shower areas	2%		2%
Unknown	6%		6%
Total	98%	99%	101%
	(116)	(12)	(128)

Table IV
Weapons Used in Homicide[a]

Firearms	6%
Cutting or stabbing weapons	75%
Blunt objects	6%
Personal weapons	2%
Strangulation	7%
Arson	4%
Other or unknown	1%
Total	101%
	(128)

[a]By *Uniform Crime Reports* Coding

Table V

Comparison of Weapons used in Prison Homicides, Institutional Homicide Identified by UCR and 1973 Homicides reported by UCR[a]

Weapons	Prison Homicides	UCR Institutional Homicides	UCR Homicides
Cutting or stabbing weapons	79%	57%	60%
Blunt objects	7%	17%	14%
Personal weapons	2%	13%	13%
Strangulation	7%	9%	5%
Arson	4%	4%	2%
Other or unknown	2%	0%	6%
Total	101%	100%	100%
	(121)	(46)	(3619)

[a]Excluding firearms.

Table VI
Cause of Death

Exsanguination	36%
Shock	9%
Asphyxia	8%
Head injuries	6%
Burns	2%
Unknown	39%
Total	100%
	(128)

Table VII

Primary Motive by Victim Status

Motive	Inmate	Guard	Inmate/Guard Total
Racial	4%	8%	5%
Nonracial	71%	41%	68%
Unknown	23%	50%	26%
Total	98%	99%	99%
	(116)	(12)	(128)

Table VIII

Percentages of Inmate or Staff Homicides by Racial Homogeneity

	Race of Victims			
	Inmate		Guard	
Race of Assailants	White	Non-White	White	Non-White
All white	56%	14%	30%	100%
All non-white	11%	49%	40%	
Mixed races	3%		20%	
One or more unkown		6%		
No assailants identified	30%	31%	10%	
Total	100%	100%	100%	100%
	(63)	(49)	(10)	(1)

29

Table IX

Comparison of Population Characteristics for Prisons
in Which Interracial Homicides Did and Did Not Occur

Characteristic		Interracial Homicide Did Occur	Interracial Homicide Did Not Occur
Percentage of	Mean	29.3	32.3
population	S.D.	16.6	21.3
under 24	N	11	21
Percentage	Mean	54.2	56.8
white	S.D.	22.4	18.5
	N	12	29
Percentage	Mean	60.5	52.8
personal	S.D.	13.1	14.6
offenders	N	10	25
Percentage	Mean	13.8	10.6
serving life or	S.D.	9.5	9.4
death sentences	N	10	25
Homicide rate	Mean	214.2	226.0
10,000	S.D.	129.2	171.6
	N	12	30

Table X

Percentage of Homicide Institutions by Percentage of Non-White Custodial Staff and by Percentages of Non-White Inmates

| | Inmates | | |
Custodial	Low Percentage	High Percentage	Difference
High percentage	60% (10)	38% (17)	22%
Low Percentage	35% (41)	24% (48)	11%
Total	39%	27%	12%

Table XI

Percentages by Race of Assailants Subjected to Action by Penal and Judicial Authorities by Race

| | | | Action | | |
Race	Prison Discipline	Referred to Prosecutor	Indicted for Murder or Lesser Offense	Found Guilty of Murder or Lesser Offense	N
White	75%	69%	63%	36%	73
Black	83%	81%	81%	33%	59
Other[a]	88%	50%	50%	0%	16

[a]Of Spanish decent except for one Indian.

CHAPTER THREE

Characteristics of Homicide Participants

INMATE/INMATE HOMICIDES

In this section, inmate/inmate homicide will be examined in greater detail, with special attention given to the characteristics of the victims and their assailants.

Inmate slayings of other inmates were the most common type of prison homicide in 1973. In 78 inmate deaths, other inmates were identified as the suspected assailants. There were 20 homicides where no suspected assailant of an inmate was identified, but reports indicated that the assailants were believed to be inmates. In an additional 15 inmate deaths, there was no indication of the status of the assailants; for the purposes of this study, however, these will be considered inmate/inmate homicides. Hence, this section deals with 113 separate homicides, with 113 victims, and with 128 identified assailants.

In 49 of the 78 cases where assailants were identified, there was a single suspect. Seventy-nine assailants were accused in the remaining 29 homicides. Two inmate assailants were identified in 19 cases. In 7 instances, 3 were accused. There were 2 cases with 5 assailants, and 1 with 6. In 1 case, 7 assailants were named. These figures reflect the numbers of suspected assailants identified and not necessarily the number of assailants who committed the crime.[1]

The immediately related milieu for inmate/inmate homicides varies considerably among those events with single assailants, those with more than one, and those with no identified assailants. The three leading "motives" recorded for single-assailant events were homosexuality, arguments and debts. These account for 65% of the primary motives in single-assailant cases. In multiple-assailant events, reprisal for "snitching" was the predominant motive, followed by gang phenomena, drug quarrels and homosexuality. These four motives encompass 67% of all multiple-assailant motives. For the cases with no identified assailants, the distribution of motives approximates the distribution for multiple-assailant events. In these events, quarrels over intoxicants were the most common motives, followed by "snitch" control and property quarrels. These motives account for 68% of those cases with identified motives but no identified assailants.

Single-assailant events seem to stem from personal involvements, while multiple-assailant events appear to be oriented more toward maintenance of the inmate social order, e.g., suppressing tendencies to inform or maintaining the quality or quantity of drugs. There is additional support for this contention in the resemblance between the motives for unidentified assailants and multiple-assailant events. In remaining unidentified, assailants may, to some extent, be protected by the inmate community.

Fifty-six percent of all events in which a single assailant was identified were considered to have been victim-precipitated. Victims slain by more than one identified inmate or by unidentified assailants precipitated their own deaths in 14% and 18% of the cases, respectively. The predominance of personal motives in single-assailant events suggests reciprocity of animosity between the adversaries. In multiple-assailant and unidentified-assailant events the victim seemed to play a more passive role.

Single-assailant events occurred much less often in the victim's cell than did multiple-assailant events. Single-assailant events tended to occur throughout the prison, which may be related to what appears to be their more spontaneous nature. Multiple assailants seemed to seek out their victims in the victim's cell rather than in the "common areas" outside the cell block. Events where assailants remained unidentified occurred in living and recreational areas.

In inmate/inmate homicides, stabbing was the predominant method of inflicting death. Multiple assailants used stabbing and strangulation exclusively. Single assailants used a wider variety of weapons, lending some additional support to the notion that one-on-one homicides were more spontaneous. Unidentified assailants used stabbing to the same extent as multiple assailants, but also used a variety of other weapons, including two handguns.

The distributions of single- and multiple-assailant events by time of day are nearly identical except for some slight differences in the proportion of homicides occurring in the evening. Nearly half of those events where assailants were identified occurred in the afternoon. In contrast, homicides having unidentified assailants were more evenly distributed through the day.

There is a strong tendency for multiple-assailant homicides to occur on weekends. Proportionately more single-assailant events occurred on weekdays than did multiple-assailant events. Events for which no assailants were identified occurred throughout the week, with Sunday, Thursday and Friday being the most common days. Homicides occurring on Saturdays almost always had suspects identified.

Comparisons of the characteristics of participants in homicide events on selected penological, criminological and demographic variables were effected in two ways. Marginals for all variables describing the different groups of participants were screened to eliminate those variables which contained large numbers of missing cases, which contained no substantial variation, or for which there was substantial evidence to suggest that the data were qualitatively poor. The original list of more than fifty variables was reduced to eighteen. Among the variables discarded were the several dealing with medical and psychiatric records of the participants. Medical histories were highly variable as to their contents and completeness. Psychiatric records suffered from a number of deficiencies, including nonstandardizable terminology and evidence that in some states having a psychiatric profile was highly correlated with having a minority status.

These eighteen variables were then used to construct simple aggregate percentage profiles for each of the desired comparisons: (1) victims and assailants; (2) victims of single assailants, victims of multiple assailants, and victims of unidentified assailants; (3) single and multiple assailants; (4) inmate assailants of inmates and inmate assailants of guards. Simple correlations were run to determine those characteristics for which there were differences. Multiple discriminant analysis was used to check these results against a further subset of the variables, several of which had been dummy-coded.

Demographically, assailants and victims can best be distinguished by marital status and age and to a lesser extent by grades completed and religion. Victims were more likely than assailants to have been married, to be older by about three years on the average, to have completed ten or more years of education, and more likely to be Protestant. The two groups were similar in terms of urban residential patterns, race, intelligence, achievement levels, work experience and military record.

In the aggregate, assailants appear to be more violent than their victims. Indications of this are to be found in the prior records of assailants, which show them proportionately to be more likely to have had a background which includes a serious personal offense. That one-quarter of the assailants were imprisoned for killing another human being compared to 18% of the victims lends further credence to the violence hypothesis. Still further confirmation is inferred from the fact that one-half of the assailants were serving time for other serious crimes against the person while, at the time of the homicide event, somewhat fewer of the victims were incarcerated for serious personal crimes. Finally, the prison records of assailants usually reflected one or more assaultive events during their incarceration, and this included 15 individuals who had previously committed homicide in prison. Victims were less likely to have been reprimanded for an assaultive event, although 5 of the victims had participated in an earlier prison homicide event.

Assailants were more likely to be first-termers, while victims were more likely to have served two or more prison terms. Although a greater proportion of assailants were serving sentences of forty or more years, they were not more likely than victims to be serving life sentences. Victims were sentenced slightly more often to terms of less than a decade. By and large, the victims had been in prison for shorter periods of time than their assailants, with nearly half of the victims having served a year or less. More than 60% of the assailants had been in the institution in excess of a year. The shorter period of incarceration of victims may help to explain the lower incidence of prison assaultive behavior described in the previous paragraph.

One of the most powerful distinctions running through the data is that between events with multiple assailants and those with single assailants. In the aggregate, the characteristics of the participants in these two types of events also differ. Multiple assailants were more likely to be Catholic, to be younger by about two years on the average, to be urban by birth and residence, to have more often completed the sixth grade, to have scored higher on standard achievement tests, and to be less likely to have below-average intelligence. Multiple assailants were slightly more likely to have served in the armed forces and were less likely to have been unfavorably discharged. There were no differences with respect to race and work experience.

The criminal histories of single and multiple assailants are not so disparate as those of victims and assailants generally, nor is there a distinctive pattern of personal violence. The two groups were about equally likely to have had prior records of serious personal offenses, to be property offenders, to be serving life sentences, to have had records of assaultive behavior while in prison, and to have been incarcerated for a year or less. However, the mean length of incarceration for single assailants exceeds that of multiple assailants by about a year, with a relatively high standard deviation, indicating an older group of single assailants in addition to a substantial younger group. Multiple assailants were more likely to have had a history of burglary and other serious property crimes, to be first-termers serving long sentences, to have been serving time for other serious personal crimes such as robbery at the time of the homicide event, and to have been previously involved in a prison homicide.

The analysis of single and multiple assailants can be paralleled with an analysis of the characteristics of the victims of single and multiple assailants. A larger proportion of the victims of multiple assailants were under age twenty-five, were white, and were somewhat more likely to be Protestant. There is little difference between victims of single and multiple assailants with respect to marital status and the proportion born in urban places. However, victims of multiple assailants were much more likely than those of single assailants to have been urban residents at the time of their incarceration. Victims of single assailants were somewhat more likely to be of below-average intelligence, were less likely to have entered the eleventh grade, and were much more likely to have achieved at the grammar school level than were victims of multiple assailants. The proportions of single-assailant victims and multiple-assailant victims having worked primarily as laborers are dramatically different. This may be a function of age. There is little difference between the military records of the two groups of victims whose assailants were identified.

The aggregate criminal records of the two groups show few differences in terms of predominant criminal record. In both instances, slightly more than one-third had been personal offenders, while approximately another third had been property offenders. Victims of multiple assailants were somewhat more likely to be serving their first prison term, while better than one-half of the victims of single assailants were hard-core recidivists. Thirty-one percent of those killed by multiple assailants were serving a sentence for homicide, compared to a smaller percentage of victims of single assailants. Multiple-assailant victims were more often guilty of serious crimes against the person. The larger percentage of victims serving life sentences were from the multiple-assailant category.

Victims of single assailants were less likely to have been in the facility for more than one year. Four victims of multiple assailants had killed in prison. One single-assailant victim was the only other victim known to have committed a prison homicide. One-third of the victims of single assailants had records of assaultive rule infractions while in prison, compared to nearly half of the victims of multiple assailants who had incurred assaultive infractions while behind bars. About 30% of both victim categories with identified assailants were known to have engaged in homosexual activities while in prison.

One way of understanding something about homicide events where the assailants remain unidentified is to ascertain how the victims of unidentified assailants compare with the victims of single and multiple assailants. We found that, in the aggregate, victims of unidentified assailants were most similar to the victims of single assailants.

The victims of unidentified and single assailants had similar proportions of whites, of Protestants, and of persons with below-average intelligence. Equivalent percentages of both groups were first-termers and recidivists. Identical proportions of both groups (57%) were incarcerated for serious personal crimes. There was no difference between the two groups with respect to the proportion serving life sentences or with respect to their records of assaultive behavior in prison.

There was no difference between the three types of victims with respect to the proportion born in an urban area and their predominant prior criminal records. Of the three groups of victims, those whose assailants went unidentified were most likely to be serving short sentences of less than ten years and were least likely to have been in the prison for more than one year. Victims of unidentified assailants could also be distinguished from those of identified assailants by the much larger proportions that had been married and served in the military. Considerably fewer of the victims of unidentified assailants had manifested homosexual behavior in prison.

The victims of unidentified assailants fell between those of single and multiple assailants with respect to the proportion under the age of twenty-five and the proportion resident in an urban area prior to incarceration. In grade completion and achievement, the victims of unidentified assailants fell between the two other groups but were somewhat closer to victims of multiple assailants. The situation is similar with respect to the proportion having been primarily employed as laborers.

This section might best be concluded by pointing out an anomaly for which we do not have an explanation. The reader may recall from earlier sections that the event characteristics for homicides with no identified assailants paralleled the event characteristics for multiple-assailant events. However, the personal characteristics of the victims of unidentified assailants most closely resemble those of the victims of single assailants. One possibility is that these findings simply point out the tenuousness of this type of approach to the data. If unresolved homicides are committed by groups, the profile of the victims of multiple assailants would be altered so as to make victims appear to be much more homogeneous. However, on the face of it, it would seem less likely that a group of assailants could remain unidentified as easily as a single individual. It could be that unresolved homicides represent a special class of premeditated homicides.

A selection of actual cases taken from the data may serve to illustrate several of the types of homicide discussed in this chapter. The first case is an instance where no assailant was identified. The second and third cases involve single inmate assailants of inmates, the former being one of the rare cases where race appears to be a motive and the latter resulting from an unspecified personal conflict. The fourth and fifth cases also involve single inmate assailants of inmates but are characterized by the motive most common to single-assailant slayings—homosexuality. The sixth and seventh cases involve multiple inmate assailants of inmates and seem to be characterized by the motive most common to multiple-assailant homicides—punishment for violation of an inmate social code.

Case 1

This homicide occurred in the maximum security section of a federal prison on a Friday in March. The time and location of the assault were unknown, and it was impossible to determine what weapons had been present, still less the motive or whether the victim had precipitated the attack in any way. The number and status of any witnesses were also unknown.

The homicide investigation was referred to the FBI, but no assailants were identified. An autopsy was performed, and there were negative findings on the presence of alcohol, drugs or brain damage. Since there was no death certificate, the cause of death and of inflicting death were also unknown.

The victim, admitted to the institution in 1968, and transferred to the maximum security area four months before the homicide, was a 51-year-old black Baptist who had never married. His IQ was 53, and although he had completed sixth grade his achievement level was unknown. He was born in a rural area but was resident in an urban one, working as a laborer.

He had previously been arrested ten times for burglary, larceny and intoxication, and had served three prior prison terms. His age at first arrest and first commitment was unknown. At the time of the homicide, he was serving a sentence of fourteen years for housebreaking and robbery. During this commitment, he had been cited for an attempted escape and for the manufacture and possession of alcohol. His usage of drugs was unknown.

The information on the family of the victim was slight. His parents had both been present in the household while he was growing up. His father worked as a shoe repairer, his mother as a domestic servant. He had six siblings. There were no records of arrests or alcohol abuse within the family. Their mental health and involvement with drugs were unknown.

Case 2

This homicide took place in the late afternoon of a Sunday in September. The assailant was white and prejudiced against blacks. The victim was black and known to the assailant. While they were opposite the office of a guard, the assailant accused the victim of previously making threats and—pushing him down the stairs—stabbed him. The assailant was not injured. There were numerous witnesses, including correctional officers and inmates. The incident was referred to the state police, and the assailant was immediately placed in administrative segregation.

This same assailant was maintained in segregation in the same institution where he was one of four assailants in another homicide on a Monday afternoon in December.

Here, too, the primary motive for the homicide was racial: four inmates assaulted a black lieutenant who had been employed at the institution for fifteen years. The assailants broke up a chair and beat the officer with the pieces; they also kicked him. The victim died of a crushed skull and internal injuries. There were no witnesses. The homicide was referred to the state police, and the four assailants were prosecuted. Three of the four, including the one who had previously committed a homicide in the same institution, were transferred to another institution.

The common assailant in these two homicides was a 25-year-old married Protestant of average intelligence. He had completed ninth grade and achieved at an eighth-grade level. His birthplace was unknown, and he resided in a rural area. He had no military record and had worked as an equipment operator and laborer. He had been arrested twelve times, starting at age 15, and had served three previous prison terms, beginning when he was 16. His prior offenses escalated from delinquency through larceny to armed robbery. The offense at the time of the homicide was aggravated assault and battery, and armed robbery with violence, carrying a sentence of six to sixteen years. He had been in the prison since March of 1969 and during that time had made three escape attempts and assaulted another prisoner

The family background showed that two brothers and his father had served prison terms for assault and battery; both parents had records of alcohol abuse. Both the mother and father were present in the household during his formative years. His father was a truckdriver. Neither the parents nor the three siblings had any record of mental health problems or drug abuse.

Case 3

This homicide took place in the middle of a Thursday afternoon in November. Both the victim and the assailant were armed. The assault took place on a walkway on the prison grounds in the presence of several correctional officers and another inmate. The information presented here is taken from the assailant's statement to prison authorities.

The assailant and victim had quarreled earlier in the day, and the victim had struck the assailant. At that time, both had knives. During the afternoon, the assailant saw the victim heading to a prison office with two correctional officers and, assuming some complaint might be filed against him, decided to intercept the group. He stepped up to the officers, stabbed the victim, who was between them, and grabbed the victim's knife from his pocket, using it to hold the other observers at bay. Eventually he was subdued and freely made a statement before being sent to lockdown. He was not injured in the attack, and a year later he was convicted and sentenced for second-degree murder.

The victim died approximately thirty minutes after the attack. The death certificate and autopsy showed the cause of death as exsanguination due to laceration of the superior vena cava.

The assailant and victim were both black Protestant, the assailant single and the victim legally separated. The assailant was fifteen years older and had been in that prison for twenty years. Both had served in that institution before their present commitment. They were both born in, and residents of, urban areas, had no military experience, and were in good health. The IQ of the assailant was unknown, but although he had completed fifth grade he was practically illiterate. The victim was of above-average intelligence, had completed seventh grade and achieved at a seventh-grade level. Both had worked as laborers, the victim having also been an equipment operator.

Their criminal histories differed: the victim had one previous adult arrest and commitment, both at age fourteen, for burglary, whereas the assailant had had five previous adult arrests and five commitments, for murder and attempted aggravated rape, as well as a juvenile commitment. The victim was in minimum custody, serving a six-year sentence for aggravated battery; the assailant was also in minimum custody, serving a life sentence for murder.

The family background material was sparse for both. The victim's father was not present in the home, and the mother worked. He had four siblings. The marriage of the assailant's parents was intact and their occupations unknown. The assailant had eight siblings.

During their prison stays, both had been cited for regulatory offenses. There was no record of either having used drugs, although the victim occasionally used alcohol. One major difference between them was that the victim had been described four months earlier as being sociopathic. He had deliberately wounded himself during his previous prison commitment.

Case 4

This homicide occurred on a Saturday afternoon in October. The victim and assailant were in a line in the cell block, waiting to receive medication. The victim had previously pressured the assailant for homosexual favors, which had been refused, and earlier that day had assaulted him. When the two met in the medication line, the victim threatened to kill the assailant; striking first, the assailant stabbed the victim with a broken fluorescent light tube. One other inmate saw the attack.

The case was referred to the coroner, who reported death as occurring about forty minutes after the attack due to multiple stab wounds in the neck region. The assailant was found guilty by the prison disciplinary committee, but the district attorney did not prosecute due to insufficient evidence.

The assailant was a 27-year-old white, separated from his first wife. He was of average intelligence and had completed seventh grade. Only the state in which he was born was known; there was no information on his residence prior to prison. He had served in the Navy before gaining a medical discharge, but his work experience was unknown.

His criminal record showed twenty-three arrests, the first at age sixteen for vagrancy, drunkenness and hit-and-run. This was his first prison commitment, begun at age twenty-three; he was serving five years to life for first-degree robbery. He had entered the prison (although not the system) in late August, 1973, and was in medium security.

He had a record of excessive alcoholism and heroin addiction, and had been diagnosed as suffering from an organic brain syndrome (psychotic, with a passive-dependent character disorder). A few days before the homicide, he had been seen by a psychiatric department member, who found him to be hallucinating and diagnosed him as psychotic.

The assailant came from a disorganized family situation. His Catholic parents had divorced, and he was raised in foster homes and orphanages. Of the three siblings, one brother was in prison on burglary charges. There was no information on the mental health or the alcohol or drug abuse of other family members.

Case 5

This homicide took place on a Tuesday afternoon in February in a classroom in the vocational building.

The victim was homosexually assaulted by three other inmates in the classroom. Another homosexual inmate, who became the assailant in the homicide, had wanted one of the assaulters for himself, and saw the victim as a rival. After the other three had left, the assailant went into the classroom and stabbed the victim, who died approximately five minutes later. An autopsy was performed; the assailant was placed in segregation, and later prosecuted and convicted for first-degree murder. The three inmates who had sexually assaulted the victim were not directly connected to the homicide.

The assailant was a 20-year-old single white Methodist, born in a rural area, who had most recently resided in an urban area. He was of average intelligence, had completed ninth grade and achieved at a seventh-grade level. He had never served in the military, and his work experience was as a laborer.

He had been arrested five times, beginning at age sixteen, for auto theft and robbery, and had served one previous prison term. He had entered this prison one and a half years before, on a five-year sentence for malicious killing of an animal. He was in maximum security and had received citations for fighting and possession of a razor. He did not use drugs but did use alcohol excessively. During the previous commitment, he had been diagnosed as possessing psychopathic traits.

The parents were married, and both were at home. The father was a disabled veteran and an alcoholic. Although there were no indications of drug abuse or mental health problems, the three brothers had all served prison terms for murder or manslaughter.

Case 6

This homicide occurred in the main recreation yard shortly before noon on a Saturday in August. The three assailants killed another member of their gang, or clique, stabbing him with two prison-made knives which were found at the scene.

The victim and assailants were all Mexicans, members of a group named

The New Family. The victim had angered the leaders of the group by not completing an assignment and by talking too much; the group's leaders had therefore ordered the assailants to assault him.

The case was referred to a coroner for a death certificate and autopsy; death was due to a severed neck artery and internal hemorrhaging into both lungs.

There was one inmate eyewitness to the assault. He was investigated by the prison disciplinary committee and found not guilty, although he had apparently acted as an observer or lookout. The other two assailants were found guilty by the prison authorities and given five days in isolation; in no case did the district attorney have sufficient information to prosecute.

Case 7

This homicide took place early on a Saturday afternoon in May. The victim was killed after only five days in the prison because he was deemed to be a police informer. Five assailants attacked the victim in the maximum security cell block during a time when the population could wander about freely. He was stabbed with a pick-type instrument which was found at the scene, strangled with a cord, stuffed in a barrel with sheets and set on fire. The victim was pronounced dead approximately two and a half hours later.

According to the coroner's report and autopsy report, the cause of death was asphyxia, although the body contained 170 stab wounds.

The homicide was also referred to the state police, and all the assailants were prosecuted. Two of the assailants were placed in protective custody for testifying against the others. Two of the assailants were brothers-in-law and were also co-defendants on a breaking and entering charge. Four of the assailants had a history of assaults in prison. The fifth assailant had been classified as having a high violence potential and was at the time under sentence for armed robbery.

INMATE/GUARD HOMICIDES

Eleven cases of correctional staff members being killed by inmates were reported to our office prior to the analysis of data.[2] These 11 inmate/guard homicides will be outlined and discussed in this section. It has been noted previously that better than four-fifths of the inmate/guard homicides were by stabbing. One other was by beating; another was performed with a handgun smuggled into the prison by another guard. For the most part, the motives for these homicides were unknown or listed as being retaliation against authority. In 1 case, it was known that the guard and his assailant had been arguing; in another case, racial tensions in the prison were focused on a black lieutenant. No cases of guard homicide were victim-precipitated. Nearly two-thirds of these homicides occurred in the cell block or in the dormitory. One each occurred in the hallway, kitchen, yard and auditorium. Nine of the victims were line officers. One was a lieutenant,[3] and 1 was a "Corrections Food Service Instructor." Two of the guards were in their second month of service at the institution; 1 was in his fifth. Three more had been at the institution longer than six months but less than one year. At the other end of the service record was a guard with twenty-six years' experience and a lieutenant with fifteen. All but 1 (the food service instructor) were assigned to custodial tasks.

The number of inmate assailants identified in inmate/guard homicides varied widely. In 4 of these cases, only 1 assailant was identified. In 6 cases, multiple assailants were named: 2 in 1 case, 3 in 2 cases, and 4 in 3 cases. In 1 case, no assailants were identified. In all, 24 assailants were named. It should be pointed out, however, that a certain amount of "double counting" occurred in arriving at this figure of 24 assailants. In a single incident, 2 guards were beaten and stabbed to death by 4 inmates confined to administrative confinement and isolation in the prison's maximum security cell block. These 4 inmates each appear twice in the data set on inmate assailants of guards.[4]

In the general description of the location of prison homicides, guard deaths tended to cluster in the summer months (65%). Three guards were killed on the same day in June—2 in a single incident at a western prison and 1 at an eastern institution. Two other guards were slain in July. A guard and a cooking instructor were stabbed to death in September. Two guards were killed in November. One guard was slain in January and 1 in December. By days of the week, the inmate/guard homicides clustered on Tuesday and Friday (72%). In those inmate/staff events where time of day was known, two-thirds were in the second twelve hours of the day.

The data gathered on staff victims of homicides were not as detailed as those on inmate victims and assailants, largely because correctional systems do not keep as detailed records on their employees as they do on their inmates. The oldest of the victims was fifty-four; the youngest was twenty-two. The median age was thirty-five years, with better than one-third of the victims being age twenty-six or younger. Racially, 10 were white, 1 was black. A ratio of 1 black custodial staff member to every 9 white guards is roughly the national race breakdown for state prisons.

Comparing those inmates who killed guards to those who killed inmates, we find that those who killed guards are more likely to be twenty-four years of age or younger. They are somewhat more likely to be white or Mexican-American and less likely to be Protestant (48% Catholic). They are somewhat less likely to have been married. They are much more likely to have been born in an urban area, but no more likely to have been an urban resident at the time of their commitment. The assailants of guards are less likely to have been of below-average intelligence, but more likely to have done poorly on grade achievement tests. There was no difference between the two groups with respect to grade completion at the tenth-grade level. Nearly a third of the guard assailants had no job experience. Only 3 of the assailants of guards had served any time in the armed services.

Comparing the criminal records of assailants of guards and assailants of inmates, it should be noted that, to a greater extent, assailants of guards had predominant prior records of serious crimes against the person. They were more likely to be first-termers, but no more likely than assailants of inmates to be recidivists. One-third were currently serving sentences for homicide—proportionately more than in the other group. Twenty-two of the 24 (91%) assailants of guards were serving sentences for serious crimes against the person. The differences between the two classes of assailants with respect to sentence are minimal, although somewhat more guard assailants were serving life terms. Assailants of guards were less likely to have been in the institution for less than one year and more likely to have a prison record of assaultive behavior in prison.

GUARD/INMATE AND GUARD/GUARD HOMICIDES

This brief section will consider the four events in the pool of 128 homicides where agents of the criminal justice system were the identified assailants. Three of these events were guard/inmate homicides. The fourth was the guard hostage accidentally shot by an officer. Given the small number of these cases, they will be discussed individually.

Each guard/inmate homicide was a case where prison guards shot inmates attempting to escape. All occurred outdoors: two in yards, the third outside the perimeter as the escapee crossed the road running in front of the facility. The two inmates killed within the fences attempted their escapes during daylight hours. The inmate who succeeded in penetrating the fence attempted his escape after dark. Only one of the inmates did not attempt a solo escape.

In all three escapes, inmates died from rifle wounds. In one event, tower guards at two posts fired twenty-one rounds from M-1 carbines at two escaping inmates, felling one with a bullet in the back. In the second event, the other inmate was shot in the head, dying instantly. In the third event, two shots were fired: a warning shot followed by a fatal wound to an unspecified region of the body.

Some attention should be given to the victims and the etiology of their escapes. The victim attempting an escape with another inmate might be described as a prison agitator in that he had a record of disciplinary infractions, including citations for inciting to riot and refusing to work. He was a drug offender who continued to take narcotics in prison. He had no previous record of violence and a very short criminal career. He had four arrests for marijuana and narcotics, with his earliest arrest at age twenty-three. He was twenty-five when he died. Prior to his criminal career, he had completed high school, earned an associate's degree and served two years in the army, from which he received an honorable discharge in 1968. He was married with a daughter and stepdaughter. At the time of his death, he was serving a sentence for attempted escape.

The inmate attempting an escape under the cover of darkness was a twenty-nine-year-old Mexican-American with a poor educational background who had a lifelong record of minor criminal offenses. He was serving his first prison term for mail theft and had been granted parole. However, he was returned to the federal correctional facility for parole violation after being charged with possession of dangerous drugs, possession of a firearm, and murder.

The third victim was a juvenile housed at an institution for adult male felons that also served as the system's medical facility.

The one case of guard/guard homicide was clearly an accident resulting from a tragic breakdown in prison security which cost two correctional officers their lives. A single inmate armed with a .25-caliber handgun took three guards hostage as part of an abortive attempt to escape. At noon, the inmate shot and killed one guard. A little over an hour later, one of the guard hostages was accidentally shot by an officer with a high-powered rifle who was trying to shoot the inmate. Within two weeks, *the New York Times* reported in regard to this incident that a correctional officer had been indicted on charges of conveying weapons into a penal institution and assisting in an attempt to escape.

Table I

A Typology of Participants in
Inmate/Inmate Homicides

Victim of single assailant	49
Victim of multiple assailants	29
Victim of unidentified assailant(s)	35
Single assailant	49
Multiple assailants	79
Unidentified assailant(s)	0

Table II

Primary Motive by Number of Assailants Identified
in Inmate/Inmate Events

Motive	Single	Multiple	None	Total
Homosexual	30%	11%	0%	17%
Debt	15%	7%	21%	14%
Gang	8%	15%	5%	9%
Drugs	0%	11%	26%	9%
Snitch	8%	29%	21%	17%
Race	10%	4%	0%	6%
Argument	20%	7%	5%	13%
Fight	7%	7%	10%	8%
Other	2%	7%	10%	6%
Total	100%	98%	98%	99%
	(40)	(27)	(19)	(86)

Table III

Proportion of Cases Victim-Precipitated by
Number of Assailants Identified
In Inmate/Inmate Events

	Assailants Identified		
Single	Multiple	None	Total
56%	14%	18%	36%
(18)	(3)	(2)	(23)

N = 64

48

Table IV

Location of Homicide by
Number of Assailants Identified
in Inmate/Inmate Events

Location	Single	Multiple	None	Total
		Assailants Identified		
Cell of participant	20%	38%	31%	28%
Cell block or domitory	31%	31%	31%	31%
Recreation areas	6%	10%	11%	9%
Hallway	8%	0%	0%	4%
Dining area	6%	3%	0%	4%
Kitchen	2%	0%	3%	2%
Training areas	4%	7%	0%	3%
Yards	8%	3%	9%	7%
Office	4%	0%	0%	2%
Shower areas	2%	3%	0%	2%
Other	6%	3%	0%	3%
Unknown	2%	0%	14%	5%
Total	99%	98%	99%	100%
	(49)	(29)	(35)	(113)

Table V

Method of Inflicting Death by
Number of Assailants Identified
in Inmate/Inmate Events

Method	Single	Multiple	None	Total
		Assailants Identified		
Stabbing	73%	83%	82%	78%
Strangulation	6%	17%	6%	9%
Beating	8%	0%	6%	5%
Burning	10%	0%	0%	4%
Shooting	0%	0%	6%	2%
Fall	2%	0%	0%	1%
Total	99%	100%	100%	99%
	(48)	(29)	(34)	(111)

CHAPTER FOUR

Characteristics of Homicide Institutions

The material prior to this chapter largely describes the characteristics of homicide events, the attributes of offenders, the attributes of victims, and the important interrelationships. In this section, homicide events are considered in relation to the milieu in which they occur. The question to be addressed is whether the physical features of prisons, the way in which prisons are organized, and the way in which prisons are run may in some way contribute to an explanation of prison homicide.

More specifically:

1. Is prison homicide related to the size of the institution, the density of the prison population, the way in which prisoners are housed, the age of the facility, the proportion of total budget spent on salaries, and/or the per capita expenditures per inmate?

2. Does the education, racial composition, and salary of staff have any bearing on whether a prison has a homicide?

3. Does the presence or absence of various types of facilities, such as libraries and recreation rooms, influence the incidence of homi-

cide? Is the frequency with which prisoners are permitted telephone, mail and visiting rights related to the incidence of homicide? How and in what ways do different sanctions for disciplinary infractions contribute to an explanation of prison homicide?

4. Do prisons with detoxification programs for alcohol and drugs and various kinds of counseling programs have fewer homicides than prisons which do not?

5. How do rehabilitative programs concerned with education, vocational training, and work- and study-release influence the incidence of homicide?

The findings presented below are based on a series of tables prepared for this project by the Bureau of Census. The data are from two sources. The first is a special survey of prisons and institutions undertaken by the Bureau in early 1974. These special census data were supplemented by data provided by the present study on the homicide status of the institution, the racial composition of the inmate population, the composition of the inmate population in terms of the number of personal offenders, and the composition of the inmate population with regard to the proportion serving life sentences. Henceforth, homicide institutions shall be defined as those adult, male, felon, penal institutions, of size 200 or more, which had at least one prison homicide in the calendar year 1973.

PRISON POPULATIONS AND PHYSICAL FEATURES

Knowledge of the absolute size of the inmate population of a prison, the designed capacity of a prison, the absolute number of inmates with a maximum security designation, the percentage of inmates in maximum security, the percentage of designed capacity in one-man cells, and the size of place (population) of a prison's geographical location enhance the possibility of accurately predicting a prison's homicide status.

Knowledge of the absolute size of the inmate population increases by about 60% the likelihood of correctly predicting the homicide status of an institution over purely chance predictions. Similarly, information about designed capacity increases ability to predict homicide status by about 60%. Absolute size of population and designed capacity of a prison measure the same factor; thus the ability to predict the homicide status of an institution is not enhanced by their joint use. Three additional indicators of size—authorized number of full-time payroll personnel, absolute number of full-time personnel, and absolute number of full-time custodial personnel—exhibited the same pattern of correlation. On this basis, one may conclude that larger prisons are much more likely to have a homicide than are smaller institutions.

There are several features of large prisons which might account for this likelihood. One is that there is simply a much larger number of possible relations among the inmates. A second is that large prisons are more likely to house maximum security inmates who may be more violence-prone. A third is that large prisons might be more difficult to control, either because the ratio of prisoners to guards is higher or because prisoners of different security statuses find it easier to mix together. If the last is true, there should be a higher percentage of homicide institutions among institutions housing prisoners of different statuses than among those where there are only minimum or maximum security prisoners.

There is a strong positive relation between the security status of a prison and whether or not the institution experienced a homicide. None of the minimum security institutions in the survey had homicides. Among institutions which were minimum and/or medium security prisons, only 13% had homicides. Forty-three percent of the prisons with some maximum security prisoners had a homicide. Knowledge of whether a prison has maximum security prisoners enhances the ability to predict the homicide status of a prison by about 80% over chance prediction. Homicides occur most frequently in prisons where at least some prisoners are assigned maximum security designations.

One method of determining the importance of mixing prisoners of different statuses is to compare the percentage of homicide institutions for different prisons with different proportions of maximum security inmates. The relationship between these two variables is curvilinear and regular. Prisons where the percentage of inmates having maximum security designations is more than 50%, but 80% or less, are more likely to experience a homicide than are prisons with no inmates with maximum security designations or prisons whose populations are entirely in maximum security status. Mixing prisoners with different security designations is associated with a higher likelihood of a prison having a homicide.

There is a positive correlation between size of the inmate population and the ratio of prisoners to custodial staff. Larger institutions are more likely to have high prisoner-to-staff ratios than are smaller prisons. However, there is almost no relationship between the ratio of prisoners to staff and the percentage of institutions having a homicide. This implies that the effect of size alone supersedes that resulting from the form of control simply associated with a higher ratio of guards to inmates.

However, another measure of control, the number of single-person cells within a prison, is related to the homicide status of an institution. Prisons having 51% to 75% of their capacity in one-man cells are more likely to have a homicide than are prisons without one-man cells or those which are made up almost entirely of one-man cells.

If inmates are assigned to individual cells, prisons should be able to exercise greater control over the inmates, and, conceivably, there should be less opportunity for inmates of different security statuses to mix. The data bear this out. If only those prisons where it is possible to have mixed security statuses are considered, and the possible types of status-mixing are taken into account, there is a smaller difference in the percentage of homicide institutions between types of security mixes when there is a very high proportion of inmates housed in one-man cells than when there is a lower proportion of inmates housed in one-man cells. Thus there is an interaction effect between this measure of control and the types of mix of security statuses in the inmate population. Prisons least likely to have a homicide are those with minimum and medium security populations with 75% or less of their populations in one-man cells. Institutions in which there are some maximum security prisoners and which have 75% or less of their populations in one-man cells were most likely to have had a homicide in 1973.

There has been considerable discussion of the general relation of density to various forms of social and physical pathology. It has been pointed out that there are various ways in which people can live in close proximity to one another. For instance, a person living in a high-density neighborhood can insulate himself from excessive stimuli by occupying a dwelling that has a very low unit density. In addition, of course, density itself takes various forms in the environment.

For the homicide study, there was no direct measure of the number of persons per acre available. However, it seems reasonable to assume that most prisons have fairly high area densities, and that the range of variation in such a measure would be sufficiently small so that systematic variation is unlikely.

A measure of crowding—occupancy as a measure of designed capacity—was available, but knowledge of the relative occupancy rate of a prison provides no gain in terms of a linear prediction of the homicide status of that institution. A prison is most likely to experience a homicide when it is 80% to 90% occupied. A prison is least likely to experience a homicide when its occupancy rate is between 90% and 100% of capacity. Only slight differences are found when comparing the group of prisons with an occupancy rate of higher than 80% with those with lower occupancy rates.

Thus, crowding does not appear to be systematically associated with prison homicide.

There has been some suggestion that older prisons may be less adequate in terms of environment than newer prisons and that this inadequacy of environment may somehow be associated with social pathology. Two different measures of the age of the institution can be utilized to give an indication of whether the age of the facility is related to its homicide status. When homicide status is related to the percentage of cells over seventy-five years of age, there is a low positive association. Knowledge of the percentage of the cells over seventy-five years of age enhances the ability to predict the homicide status of an institution by about 15% over chance guesses.

The relationship between age of the facility site and an institution's homicide status is irregular. Knowledge of the age of the facility site increases by 25% the ability to predict the homicide status of an institution over simple knowledge of marginals. The strength of the relationship can be increased slightly if one simply distinguishes those institutions with facility sites more than fifty years old from those with facility sites of fifty years or less. Institutions with older facility sites and larger numbers of inmates are more likely to have homicides than newer institutions with similarly large inmate populations.

However, when size is introduced as a control in the relationship between age of facility site and homicide status, there is an interesting specification. The correlation between age of facility site and the homicide status of an institution drops markedly for institutions with 1,000 or more inmates. In other words, in cases of large institutions, their size explains about half of the correlation between age of the facility site and homicide status. However, the correlation between age of facility site and homicide status remains high for institutions with fewer than 1,000 inmates. Age of the facility site appears to be an important factor in the incidence of homicide in small institutions but not in large institutions. This may reflect the fact that smaller institutions may not have the necessary finances available to undertake renovations. Unfortunately, data are not sufficient to test this proposition.

The setting in which a prison is located may influence its chances of having a homicide. The data at hand indicate that prisons located in urban areas are more likely to have a homicide than prisons in rural areas. Again, size may be a factor. Institutions in urban areas may be larger than those in rural settings. Indeed, this appears to be the case. Forty percent of the prisons with 1,250 or more inmates are located in urban areas compared to 25% of the prisons with 1,249 or fewer inmates.

Large urban prisons are more likely to have a homicide than smaller rural prisons. But large rural prisons are more likely to have a homicide than large urban prisons. Once again, there is a specification. The percentage difference in homicide institutions between large urban prisons and large rural prisons is about 12%. The same figure for small urban and rural prisons is 29%. Hence, there is an interaction effect between setting and size which suggests that for large rural prisons cultural differences between rural and urban populations are important, and that large rural prisons are probably more likely to have high percentages of inmates from urban areas.

PRISON STAFFS

The proportion of white custodial staff in most prisons is very high. In only 1 of the 130 cases was the proportion of white custodial personnel less than 50%. In well over four-fifths of the cases, the percentage of white custodial staff exceeded 90%.

A comparison of this measure of racial composition of prison staffs for homicide and non-homicide institutions indicates a low negative linear relationship. Prisons with the highest proportions of white custodial staff are least likely to have a prison homicide. Once the proportion of white custodial staff falls below 95%, the relative numbers of prisons having homicides is fairly constant. Knowledge of the proportion of custodial staff who are white enhances the ability to predict the homicide status of an institution by about 30%.

If the proportion of black custodial personnel is used as a measure of the racial composition of the staff, the relationship with homicide status is curvilinear. Proportionately, more homicides occur in prisons where the custodial staff is between 5% and 20% black than in prisons with lower or higher percentages of black custodial staff.

The relationship between the proportion of full-time non-white custodial personnel and the homicide status of an institution exhibits a curvilinear trend similar to that between the homicide status of an institution and the proportion black. Institutions where the relative number of non-white custodial personnel is 9% to 29% are more likely to have a homicide than where the percentage is greater or smaller.

It has frequently been suggested that more highly educated people tend to be less authoritarian and less rigid in their dealings with others. If this is the case, it might be expected that institutions which have higher educational standards for their custodial staffs would have fewer instances of conflict and violence between the staff and inmates. It is conceivable that this pattern of relations might also be reflected in the dealings of inmates with each other.

Of the 126 prisons for which information was available, 23% did not require a high school education for custodial staff. Prisons requiring a high school education for custodial personnel are slightly less likely to have homicide events than are those prisons which do not. However, the percentage difference is small, and knowledge of educational requirements adds little to the ability to predict the homicide status of an institution.

If the proportion of the custodial staff who meet the educational requirements is related to the homicide status of an institution, the trend for the previous finding is reaffirmed but the relationship is weak. Unfortunately, the information is not applicable or missing in some 44% of the cases, thus making it difficult to interpret the latter finding.

Likewise, when the percent of custodial personnel without a high school education is related to homicide status, there is a low negative trend. Homicides are less likely to occur in institutions where all of the custodial staff have completed high school. The proportion of missing data is too high to place much stock in an interpretation of this finding. Homicides are less likely in institutions where the custodial staff is better educated, although care should be exercised in interpreting this finding.

Requiring advanced education for wardens makes little difference in the proportions of institutions having homicides. Where the requirement is "some college or less," there is a very slight tendency for more homicides. When actual education is considered, institutions whose wardens have a college degree are more likely to have homicides than are prisons where wardens have more or less education.

These findings about the relation of education to homicide status of the institution are not necessarily surprising. Data from other studies suggest that people, regardless of their level of education, who work in authoritarian environments where they have little control over decisions tend to be authoritarian in their relations with others. Given the fact that prisons are by their very nature authoritarian, it is unlikely that education of custodial staffs would have a strong ameliorative influence on the incidence of homicide.

Although this section has been concerned mainly with the characteristics of prison personnel and concomitant variation in homicide rates, it is perhaps appropriate to conclude with some observations on per capita expenditures on inmates. The issue is whether additional expenditures per inmate may result in better facilities, more adequate rehabilitative programs, and a more adequately staffed prison, which, in turn, may have some effect on the number of homicides.

There is a curvilinear relationship between annual per capita expenditures and the percentage of homicide institutions. A higher proportion of institutions have homicides when the annual per capita operating expenses are between $3,000 and $4,999. When expenditures per prisoner fall below $3,000 or exceed $7,000, institutions are least likely to have a homicide. Unfortunately, given the data at hand, it is not possible to introduce size as a control into this relationship.

PRISON FEATURES AFFECTING INMATE MORALE

The possibility of communicating with people outside of prison could conceivably influence the morale of prisoners and, in turn, their relationships with other prisoners and custodial staff. Thus, it seems plausible that mail, telephone and visiting rights might in some way be related to whether an institution had a homicide. One possibility is that a greater frequency of such rights might have a positive effect on prisoner morale generally. Alternatively, the personal contact afforded by visits and telephone rights may be the occasions of bad news for the inmate, leading to brooding and ill temper and a feeling of helplessness and frustration as the inmate has little power to resolve the difficulty while confined.

There is almost no variation in the policies of institutions on mail rights and thus little possibility for concomitant variation with homicide status. Institutions with unlimited telephone rights are slightly less apt to have a homicide than those institutions which have them less than monthly. The relationship is irregular. Institutions with weekly visiting rights are more likely to have had a homicide than those institutions which are more or less permissive with regard to visiting rights.

At best, these findings can only be suggestive. Unlimited telephone rights may permit inmates to resolve more adequately anxieties which may result from their perceptions of what is taking place outside the walls. The curvilinear relationship with respect to visiting rights is consistent with the notion that periodic visits may induce stress. Less frequent visiting rights are less apt to upset the routine of the prison, while more frequent visiting rights may allow prisoners to keep in close touch with what is going on outside the prison. Once again, it is important to stress the speculative nature of these observations. The relationships are not strong, and the interrelationships may be a function of other considerations such as the size of the prison, the availability of personnel, and budget.

All of the prisons in our universe had facilities such as special or general purpose rooms, libraries and, with two or three exceptions, barbershops and playing fields. Thus there could be no variation with homicide status.

Gymnasiums were lacking in 38 institutions, but there were no differences in the proportions of homicide institutions. There was no relationship between the presence or absence of amenities and homicide status.

Alienation and resentment might follow from the inability of prisoners to deal effectively with their legal problems. Thus it seems reasonable that the availability of legal aid might be related to conflict. Nineteen percent of institutions had a paid staff person or persons who could help prisoners with their legal problems, while 54% had a program for volunteers to aid prisoners with their legal problems. There were no differences in the percentages of homicide institutions by whether or not payroll staff legal aid was offered, but the percentage of homicide institutions was higher among prisons with volunteer legal aid programs than among those prisons where there was none. Knowledge of whether a prison has volunteer legal aid enhances the ability to predict homicide status by about 40%.

There is no obvious reason why volunteer legal aid should be positively and directly related to the incidence of homicide. Instead, this correlation may reflect heightened levels of "class consciousness" among prisoners brought about by an increased awareness of legal rights, real or imagined, and attendant higher levels of conflict. Like some of the other observations in this chapter, this interpretation is quite speculative, but is not inconsistent with data presented earlier in the study and appears to deserve further exploration.

The use of different types of positive and negative sanctions may influence the behavior of prisoners and the quality of the social milieu in which they live. In considering different sanctions, we found little or no variation among institutions in the use of two specific types of disciplinary action. Less than 4% of the 130 institutions suspended community rights as a disciplinary measure. Just under 6% of the 130 institutions used transfer to another institution as a disciplinary measure. Given this lack of variation, differences in relative numbers of homicide institutions are uninterpretable. Suspension of visiting rights did vary between institutions in terms of its use as a disciplinary measure, but there were no differences in the relative percentages of homicide for those institutions using it and those institutions not using it as a disciplinary measure. To summarize: loss of community rights, interinstitutional transfer, and suspension of visiting rights are not related to homicide status.

There were positive associations between the homicide status of an institution and the use of four types of disciplinary measures. There were low positive relationships between the use of solitary confinement and the use of segregation for disciplinary purposes and the homicide status of an institution. Unfortunately, it is neither clear nor possible to determine from the data at hand whether some institutions use both solitary confinement and segregation or whether these disciplinary methods represent different names for the same sanction at different institutions. There is evidence—most notably the low number of institutions which use segregation and the fact that this number corresponds closely with the number of institutions not having solitary confinement—to support the latter possibility.

If these data are merged, there is a substantial positive association between the use of segregation/solitary confinement for disciplinary purposes and the homicide status of an institution. Institutions which use segregation or solitary confinement are 55% more likely than chance to have homicides.

There is also a strong correlation between restriction of privileges and the homicide status of an institution. Institutions utilizing privilege restriction as a disciplinary measure are 60% more likely than chance to have a homicide. Institutions which use extra work as a disciplinary measure are only slightly more likely to have homicides than prisons where this sanction is not employed.

There were sanctions which exhibited a negative relationship with homicide status of an institution. A smaller percentage of institutions which segregate repeat offenders have homicides than do institutions which do not segregate repeat offenders. Knowledge of whether or not an institution segregates repeat offenders enhances prediction of homicide status about 10% above chance levels.

There is a slightly stronger negative relationship between having a furlough program and the homicide status of an institution. Institutions with furlough programs are less likely to have homicides. This may in part be an artifact of the security status of the institution, although the suppressing effect of security status may not be strong.

Compared to chance expectations, institutions which use reduction of good time as a sanction are 26% less likely to have a homicide than institutions which do not use this sanction.

Finally, we looked at whether or not prisoners could appeal misconduct charges. All misconduct charges could be appealed in 99% of all institutions which were in the universe with which we were concerned. Thus there could be no differences between homicide and non-homicide institutions.

REHABILITATIVE PROGRAMS

Supposedly, one of the functions of prison is the rehabilitation of inmates. The purposes of rehabilitation programs are manifold, but it is probably safe to assume that two of the most important functions are to resocialize inmates so that they may function within the norms of the larger society and to provide inmates with skills which they may draw upon once they are released from prison. To the extent that such programs actually change the behavior and outlook of prisoners and influence the environment within which inmates and guards interact, one might expect lower levels of socially unacceptable conflict and less likelihood of homicide.

The data available to us permit the evaluation of rehabilitation in two ways. The first is to consider the ratio of inmates to rehabilitative personnel and observe how the incidence of homicide varies with this ratio. The second is to look at various types of rehabilitative programs and see if the percentage of homicide institutions varies with the presence or absence of such programs. There are numerous problems with the latter approach, for it fails to deal with the quality of such programs or the degree of participation in them. Finally, it may be that rehabilitative programs will have little impact on homicidal violence simply because those who engage in such activity are prisoners who on other grounds are less likely to commit homicide in prison.

There is a positive relationship between the ratio of inmates to rehabilitative personnel and the percentage of homicide institutions. That is, the greater the number of inmates to rehabilitative personnel, the greater the likelihood of an institution having a homicide. However, this relationship may be a function of the security status of prisons. Minimum and medium security prisons, and prisons with a low percentage of maximum security inmates, may have high concentrations of rehabilitative personnel since the inmates in such prisons are more likely to be in prison for shorter terms and to be confronted fairly immediately with the problems of reentry into society. Larger prisons, on the other hand, may have relatively fewer rehabilitative personnel simply because of size.

When the percentage of inmates in maximum security is less than 40%, there are no differences in the percentage of homicide institutions between those institutions which have fewer than 30 inmates for each staff member who has responsibilities for rehabilitation and institutions which have higher proportions of inmates to rehabilitative personnel. However, where the percentage of maximum security inmates is higher than 40%, there is a difference. Institutions with smaller ratios of inmates to rehabilitative personnel are less likely to have homicides than are institutions with higher ratios.

When size is controlled, we found that among small institutions there is no difference in the percentage of institutions having a homicide, regardless of the ratio of inmates to rehabilitative personnel. With large institutions, we found differences in the percentage of homicide institutions—those having fewer inmates to rehabilitative personnel are more likely to have a homicide than those with higher ratios of inmates to rehabilitative personnel. This latter finding came somewhat as a surprise. The data in the table showing these findings are somewhat suspect since some of the cells in the table do not meet the usual criterion for cell size. But, assuming that the relationship were to be sustained with a larger N, this finding might be partially explained by the possibility of larger budgets or the feeling on the part of correctional authorities that rehabilitative personnel are needed most in the largest prisons. In sum, it is difficult to be conclusive about the need for more rehabilitative personnel until there has been an opportunity to explore the issue more fully.

If we turn to the consideration of specific programs, we find that of the institutions in our population more than 90% offered individual counseling. Group counseling was offered at slightly fewer institutions. There was so little variation in whether or not institutions offered individual counseling that the table exhibiting the relationship of this variable with homicide status could not meaningfully be interpreted. There is a slight difference in the percentages of homicide institutions between categories of "offering" and "not offering" group counseling, but the difference is small. Prediction is enhanced by slightly more than 10%.

There was no difference in the proportion of homicide institutions between those prisons offering and not offering alcohol treatment. However, there is a slightly higher percentage of homicide institutions among those which did not offer drug treatment as opposed to those which did. Knowledge of whether an institution has a drug treatment program enhances the ability to predict the homicide status of the institution by slightly less than 20%. Thus the evidence at hand suggests that the availability of counseling and drug and alcohol treatment programs did not influence or had only minimal influence on whether or not an institution was likely to have a homicide. All of these findings must be tempered with the knowledge that issues of quality and levels of participation in rehabilitative programs have not been addressed.

EDUCATIONAL AND VOCATIONAL PROGRAMS

It was possible to compare homicide and non-homicide institutions on whether they offered various types of educational and vocational programs. First it was discovered that such high percentages of institutions offered remedial education and vocational training, well over 96% in each case, that there simply could not be any concomitant variation with the homicide status of the institution.

There was variation in whether or not institutions offered part-time study-release programs and/or work-release programs. However, there was essentially no difference in the proportions of homicide and non-homicide institutions in terms of whether or not part-time study-release was offered or whether or not a prison had a work-release program.

There was a low positive association between the homicide status of institutions and whether or not a college degree program was offered. Relatively more institutions offering the programs had homicides than did those which did not offer them. Educational programs do not relate to the homicide status of an institution or, in the case of college programs, seem to be slightly associated with the incidence of homicide.

The homicide status of institutions can also be examined in terms of whether a prison had an industry program and the rate of participation in it. Institutions which had an industry program were much more likely to have a homicide than those which did not. If an institution had an industry program, there appears to be a slightly negative relationship between rate of participation and homicide status. A slightly smaller proportion of institutions have homicides when participation in prison industry exceed 20% than is the case when participation is under 20%.

The relative numbers of homicide institutions can be compared by whether or not the institutions offer job placement. Knowledge of whether or not an institution offers job placement enhances the ability to predict the homicide status of an institution by about 60%. However, it should be pointed out that the amount of variation in offering job placement programs is small; hence care should be taken in the interpretation of this rather high degree of association.

Table I

Percentage of Homicide Institutions
By Absolute Size of Inmate Population

Size of Inmate Population		
200-499	500-999	1,000+
9%	31%	51%
(3)	(15)	(15)

N = 129

Table II

Percentage of Homicide Institutions
by Type of Security

Type of Security		
Minimum Only	Minimum and Medium	At Least Some Maximum
0%	13%	43%
(0)	(3)	(40)

N = 130

Table III

Percentage of Homicide Institutions by
Relative Percentage of Inmates in Maximum Security

Relative Percentage of Inmates in Maximum Security				
No Maximum	More than 0% but less than 50% Maximum	50% to Less than 90% Maximum	90% to Less than 100% Maximum	100%
8%	44%	64%	36%	7%
(3)	(18)	(16)	(5)	(1)

N = 130

64

Table IV

**Percentage of Homicide Institutions by
Percentage of Capacity in One-Man Cells**

Percentage of Capacity in One-Man Cells				
None	1-25%	25-50%	51-75%	76-100%
22%	29%	43%	78%	30%
(5)	(8)	(6)	(7)	(17)

N = 130

Table V

**Percentage of Homicide Institutions for Prisons Housing
Prisoners with Different Security Statuses by Type of
Mix of Statuses and Percentage of the Inmate Population
Housed in Single-Person Cells**

Percentage of single-person Cells	Minimum and medium	Minimum and/ or medium and maximum	Percentage difference
75 or Less	9%	57%	48%
	(1)	(25)	
76-100	33%	39%	6%
	(2)	(14)	
Total	18%	49%	21%
	(3)	(39)	

N = 97

65

Table VI

Ratio of Prisoners to Custodial Staff
by Size of Prison

Ratio Prisoners to Staff	Size of Prison (Number of Inmates)		
	Less than 600	600-1,250	1,250 or More
Less than 4:1	50%	27%	13%
4:1 - 6:1	23%	40%	47%
More than 6:1	27%	33%	39%
Total	100%	100%	99%
	(44)	(48)	(38)

N = 130

Table VII

Percentage of Homicide Institutions
by Ratio of Prisoners to Staff

Ratio of Prisoners to Staff		
Less than 4:1	4:1-6:1	More than 6:1
33%	36%	30%
(13)	(17)	(13)

N = 130

Table VIII

Percentage of Homicide Institutions by Type of Disciplinary Measures Used

Disciplinary Measure	Disciplinary Measure Used		N
	No	Yes	
Loss of community rights	34% (41)	0 0	126
Institutional transfer	34% (40)	14% (1)	126
Suspension of visiting rights	33% (21)	32% (20)	126
Segregation	32% (33)	36% (8)	126
Solitary confinement	26% (11)	36% (30)	126
Restriction of privileges	13% (2)	35% (39)	126
Extra work	29% (17)	36% (24)	126
Segregation of repeat offenders	37% (37)	31% (5)	117
Furlough program	38% (18)	30% (25)	130
Reduction of good time	42% (11)	30% (30)	130

67

Table IX
Percentage of Homicide Institutions by
Type of Treatment and Rehabilitation Program

Program	No	Yes	N
Individual counseling	14% (1)	34% (42)	129
Group counseling	29% (4)	34% (39)	128
Alcoholic treatment	33% (5)	33% (38)	129
Drug treatment	40% (8)	32% (35)	129
Study-release	33% (14)	33% (29)	130
Work-release	33% (25)	32% (17)	130
College program	27% (7)	35% (36)	130

Table X

Percentage of Homicide Institutions by
Type of Legal Aid Offered to Prisoners

| Type of Aid | Legal Aid Offered | | N |
	No	Yes	
Payroll staff legal aid	33% (34)	32% (8)	128
Volunteer legal aid	24% (14)	41% (29)	130

Table XI

Percentage of Homicide Institutions by
Age of Facility Site and Size of Institution

Size of Institution	Facility Less than 51 Years Old	Facility 51 or More Years Old	Percentage Difference
1,000 or more inmates	50% (14)	58% (11)	8%
999 or fewer inmates	11% (5)	33% (11)	22%
Total	45% (19)	55% (22)	10%

Table XII

Percentage of Homicide Institutions by Geographical Location and
Size of Institution

Size of Institution	Rural	Urban	Percentage Difference
Fewer than 1,250 inmates	14% (10)	43% (10)	29%
1,250 or more inmates	65% (15)	53% (8)	12%
Total	25% (23)	47% (18)	22%

N = 130

Table XIII

Percentage of Homicide Institutions by Ratio of Inmates to Full-time Rehabilitative Personnel

Ratio of Inmates to Rehabilitative Personnel	
Greater than or equal to 30:1	Less than 30:1
38%	31%
(25)	(17)

N = 121

Table XIV

Percentage of Homicide Institutions by Ratio of Inmates to Full-Time Rehabilitative Personnel Controlled for the Percentage of Inmates in Maximum Security

	Ratio of Inmates to Rehabilitative Personnel		
	Less than 30:1	Greater than or Equal to 30:1	Percentage Difference
40% or more of inmates in maximum security	36% (8)	50% (14)	14%
Less than 40% of inmates in maximum security	27% (9)	29% (11)	2%

N = 121

Table XV

**Percentage of Homicide Institutions by Ratio of Inmates to
Full-Time Rehabilitative Personnel Controlled for Size of Institution**

	Ratio of Inmates to Rehabilitative Personnel		
	Less than 30:1	Greater than or Equal to 30:1	Percentage Difference
Greater than or equal to 1,250 inmates	78% (7)	59% (16)	19%
Less than 1,250 inmates	22% (10)	23% (9)	1%

CHAPTER FIVE

Conclusions

In aggregate terms, homicide would not seem as pervasive a problem in prisons as assault. There are indications that victimization rates for homicide in prisons are less than one-twentieth those for assault. However, this should not obscure the importance of homicide in the prison community.

Our studies have shown that mortality from all causes is lower among prison inmates than the mortality of a male population of similar age composition on the outside. The probability of a prisoner dying from natural causes is about three-fifths of what it would be on the outside and about one-twentieth of what it would be from accidental causes. On the other hand, there are twice as many deaths by suicide as would be expected in terms of the general population. The actual number of homicides is about what would be expected in terms of the general population but twice what would be expected in terms of the proportion of prison deaths expected from homicide. In general, it seems reasonable to conclude that prisoners are safer from the natural causes of death and accidents than men outside the walls. Prisoners, as opposed to a similar population outside the walls, are exposed to higher risks of suicide. There is little evidence in this study which might contribute to an explanation of the high suicide rate, although it is tempting to speculate about the conduciveness of the penal milieu to self-destructive melancholia.

It is not possible to determine conclusively why prisoners are the victims of homicide as often as their counterparts outside the walls, because there is no parallel study of homicide in the general population. However, we can be definitive about the patterns of homicide in prison. Perhaps the most important question is whether homicidal acts stem from the influences of physical, social and cultural environments in prisons or whether acts of homicide can largely be explained in terms of the characteristics of the individuals involved. The most appropriate answer seems to be that these factors are interactive.

Size, not density, appears to be the most important environmental influence. Indeed, density runs a poor second as an explanatory factor. The simplest and most straightforward interpretation of these findings is that large prisons are more likely to have people who engage in violent and aggressive behaviors. There is some evidence to suggest a selective factor at work in terms of who is admitted to which prison. Further, it may be more difficult to exercise control in large prisons due to the sheer numbers of people involved. It is known that while the numbers of staff increase in linear fashion with the number of prisoners, the total number of interactions which are possible increases geometrically. The covariation of the ratio of prisoners to custodial staff and size is not matched by covariation between the ratio of prisoners to custodial staff and homicide status. The implication is that more guards will not necessarily lead to greater control and fewer homicides. At this point, there is a strong temptation to suggest a need for smaller prisons, but this should perhaps be resisted until more is known about the social processes in and the selective factors contributing to the composition of prisons large and small.

The institutional section of this report describes several findings bearing on other aspects of the physical environment of prisons, such as the availability of recreational facilities. There was no relationship between the presence or absence of these sorts of facilities and whether or not the institution had a homicide. Several words of caution are in order. There is no indication in the data as to the quality of these facilities or the extent to which they might be used or are available to prisoners who commit homicides. Furthermore, the reader should be warned against inferring anything about the importance of such services in terms of social situations other than homicide events.

The evidence on cultural influences is mixed. Regional differences in homicide mortality rates exist, although determining the precise sociocultural influences which are at work is beyond the scope of this study. Prisons located in urban areas are more likely to have homicides than those in rural areas. The rural-urban distinction shows up in the profiles of single and multiple assailants, with single assailants being more rural in their residence patterns than multiple assailants. Likewise, the victims of single assailants are more rural in their residence patterns than are the victims of multiple assailants.

The media have drawn much attention to the presumed interracial nature of many prison conflicts. While the evidence at hand indicates that this concept may have some validity in some state prison systems, race is not a major factor in prison homicide when prisons are considered in the aggregate nation-wide.

In the mortality section of this study, it was reported that blacks and whites were victimized in proportion to their numbers in the prison population. Given the fact that young blacks outside prison walls are twelve times as likely to be victimized by homicide, the racial parity of victimization within prison walls is striking. Anything that might be construed to be a "subculture of violence" among blacks outside prison appears to be ameliorated by conditions inside prison walls. Whites on the inside are victimized in greater numbers than on the outside.

Fewer than 8% of all homicides were reported to have stemmed from interracial tension. When the race of the participants is considered, about one-tenth of the inmate-homicide events and slightly under one-half of the staff-homicide events involved an assailant or assailants of one race and a victim of another. The higher number of interracial events for guards may reflect the fact that in nearly 80% of the prisons surveyed, 80% of the guards were white. Four of the 5 guard victims of interracial events were white.

Several caveats are in order. Events involving mixed racial groups of assailants may not have originated from racial motivations. Some events with racially homogeneous participants may have had racial motivations, and events in which victims and assailants were racially heterogeneous may have been inspired by circumstances other than race. The fact remains, however, that no more than one-eighth of all 1973 homicide events could be identified as interracial.

Although the full implications of the data have yet to be explored, there is a relationship between the racial composition of the staff and whether an institution had a homicide. Although the finding may simply reflect the geographical location of prisons, prisons whose custodial staffs are almost entirely white were less apt to have had a homicide. Prisons with staffs that are 5% to 20% black are more likely to have homicides than when there is a smaller or a larger proportion of black custodial staff. This may reflect prisons which have experienced racial conflict and are in a transitional period, attempting to come to grips with staffing problems.

The data base permits the exploration of the relations between a number of other aspects of social environment and prison homicide. Prisons with better-educated custodial staff and higher per capita expenditures on prisoners are slightly less likely to have homicides. The data are quite consistent on these points, but for some variables the proportion of missing data is sufficiently great to warrant considerable care in interpretation.

It is not surprising that various types of education, work- and study-release programs show no strong variation with the homicide status of an institution. The people who commit prison homicides are not likely to be prisoners who perceive that they might derive immediate benefits from such programs. The positive relationship between prison industry programs and homicide status may be confounded by size, which has previously been shown to be potent for identifying homicide institutions. Size may also account for the relationship between types of rehabilitative programs and homicide.

Once again, several words of caution are necessary with regard to rehabilitative programs and their relation to homicide. The data indicate the presence or absence of a program and not its quality or the rate of participation therein. Furthermore, the data should not be construed to mean that these programs may not have a salutatory effect on other kinds of violence and conflict.

Several interesting relationships were identified between types of disciplinary measures used by institutions and whether an institution experienced a homicide. The combination of solitary confinement and segregation was positively associated with homicide. Likewise, restriction of privileges showed a strong positive association with prison homicides. Discipline by the reduction of good time was negatively associated with prison homicide.

The positive relationship between volunteer legal aid and the homicide status of an institution might suggest a relationship between the collective consciousness of prisoners, their concerns about rights, and the levels of prison violence. In any future study, it would be valuable to find some way of adequately studying this dimension of prison life.

Distinguishing between single- and multiple-assailant events proved to be one of the most powerful ways of differentiating homicide events. There are several findings which lead us to believe that single-assailant events are more spontaneous and personal, while multiple-assailant events represent attempts to maintain the social order of the prison community. Personal circumstances such as quarrels involving homosexuality, arguments and debts most frequently characterize single-assailant events. Informers, gangs and drugs were frequently cited as circumstances for multiple-assailant events. Single-assailant events were much more likely to have been reported as victim-precipitated than were multiple-assailant events. Single-assailant events occurred throughout the prison and a broader range of weapons were used, making these homicides appear more episodic. Multiple-assailant events occurred more often in the living quarters and were more often carried out with the most efficacious weapon available, the knife. The planning necessary to organize multiple assailants and secure a suitable weapon implies premeditation. Some of the descriptions of multiple-assailant events have an almost ritualistic quality, reflecting a need to express solidarity.

Little has been said about homicides with staff as victims. Staff members are less than half as likely as inmates to be victimized. There is minimal information available about the personal characteristics of staff-victims. Unlike inmate events, which are fairly evenly distributed in time, staff homicides occur more often in the summer. Whether this represents a case of the "long hot summer" syndrome or whether it is an artifact of the small number of cases cannot be determined. In roughly half of the cases, the staff-victim had been employed at the institution less than a year. Many victims, staff and inmate, had been incarcerated in the prison for their current offense or employed at the prison for less than a year, respectively. This might suggest that some of these deaths represent cases of inadequate socialization to prison life.

More than half of the assailants had predominant prior criminal records of armed assault, robbery, rape or homicide, while a quarter were currently serving sentences for homicide. Over three-quarters were imprisoned for some serious personal crime. The resolution of conflict by physical violence was a trademark of many of these men before their present incarceration. Likewise, the victims were often men with a violent past. More than one-third had prior records of personal violence. Nearly two-thirds were being punished for violent crimes. Given the expectation that the two groups would differ, the similarities are striking. In many single-assailant inmate/inmate events, chance factors appear to have determined who emerged the victim. Unfortunately, because of problems in standardizing the data, we were not able to determine how assailants and victims differ from the general prison population.

Once in prison, the assailants and victims generally continued to be violent. Nearly 40% of the victims had been reprimanded at the prison for assaultive behavior, while more than 60% of the assailants of inmates had assaultive prison disciplinary infractions. Four-fifths of the assailants of guards had been cited for acts of personal violence while in prison.

These findings lend support to the position that the immediate source of violence is the individual as opposed to the general milieu. The environment may be an important mediator of behavior, but there is substantial validity in the representation of prison homicides as violent acts by violent men. In addition, as prisons are supposed to be institutions for control of such men, homicides represent occasions when that control breaks down. One of the strongest relationships in the study was that between homicide and whether a prison had at least some maximum security prisoners. The highest proportion of institutions having homicides were those where minimum and/or medium security inmates were housed in institutions with maximum security inmates. This relationship remained even after size was taken into account. Furthermore, it has been shown that housing prisoners in single-person cells is related to less likelihood of having a homicide. Both of these findings suggest that certain types of control are important.

Unfortunately, beyond these measures and the ratio of inmates to staff cited earlier, there is little in our data to index other forms of control. Control is a very difficult concept to operationalize. The amount of "lockdown" time might provide a first approximation, but it undoubtedly varies throughout the course of the year in any prison, and its causal status is difficult to determine. Beyond this, physical manifestations of control and formal sanctions may or may not be related to the psychological climate of control which exists in the penal milieu.

Some attention should be drawn to the institutional response to the homicide and to the disposition of individual assailants. The status of the victim seems to precondition the investigative response and subsequent treatment of alleged assailants by the judicial system. Coroners were consulted less often in the cases of guard victims. This may simply indicate that inmates are more apt to die unattended by a physician. Autopsies were performed equally for both groups of victims. Differing modes of investigating prison homicides resulted in differing rates of success in identifying alleged assailants and in developing sufficient evidence to lead to indictments and convictions. State police forces showed the best overall record in homicide clearances, indictments and convictions; the FBI showed the worst. Prison officials alone can almost always identify suspects, but cases which go to the grand jury without outside investigative assistance do poorly and seldom result in a conviction. It appears that police agencies which might seem to have the most experience investigating homicide generally should be used to investigate prison homicides. This experience pays off in higher rates of clearance, indictments and conviction.

Cases of guard homicide are followed more often by indictments but no more often by convictions than are inmate homicides. Black assailants are more often identified and indicted than white assailants. However, the outstanding fact is that only slightly more than one-quarter of all cases of prison homicide result in convictions. Given the closed environment in which these homicides occur, one might expect this rate to be higher. However, it should be kept in mind that the very cohesiveness, the violation of which might have resulted in a multiple-assailant homicide, may likewise effectively prevent the production of evidence sufficient for conviction. Furthermore, the public fear in the case of an unsolved homicide in the outside community—leading to pressure for solution and conviction—would understandably not exist for a prison homicide. After all, whatever is unknown about the inmate assailant, at least one is aware that he is already confined.

SOME POLICY RECOMMENDATIONS

Size, security status and—to a much lesser extent—density are important correlates of prison homicide. Size undoubtedly obscures a number of social processes. In the light of budgetary constraints, it is probably naive to think in terms of significantly decreasing the size of prisons, although this appears to be desirable. Rather, attention and resources might more profitably be focused on control. Maximum security prisoners should be isolated and treated differently from prisoners of other security statuses. Different operating procedures and schedules should correspond to different levels of security.

Some small benefits might accrue from hiring custodial staff with greater amounts of education, although more dramatic gains might come from evaluation of staff in terms of their ability to perceive potential violence and, while attaining empathy with prisoners, not to compromise their positions as agents of control.

We have shown that past evidence of violent behavior is the best indicator of future violent action. The offender's assaultive disciplinary infractions and general criminal record of violence should be weighed heavily in determining his security status. Static assessments of violence potential made at the time of admission should be avoided. Violence potential and security status of prisoners should constantly be reassessed and changed as conditions warrant.

Identification of prisoners with backgrounds of personal violence should be further augmented with a tracking system which allows for the exchange of information within and between correctional systems on such prisoners.

As a practical matter, there is probably little that can be done to prevent episodic homicides. However, more attention to gang activity, to the availability and use of alcohol and drugs, and to special precautions for inmates identified by the prison community as informers might serve to reduce premeditated homicides.

Further research efforts would undoubtedly be enhanced by a more uniform and centralized record-keeping system. Any system of record-keeping used in the study of homicide should be designed for that specific purpose and should include information which is not normally kept for administrative purposes.

No piece of research can, or ought, to stand in isolation from the continuing trends of study in related areas. It would seem appropriate, therefore, to suggest those areas of the present study which might best give rise to other research efforts and what direction these might take.

One of the principal findings of the study is that there appear to be two distinguishable types of prison homicide: single-assailant homicide and multiple-assailant homicide. The first seems to be more spontaneous, more often victim-precipitated, and motivationally characterized by homosexuality. As such, it seems to parallel in many of its features the common "domestic" homicide outside of prison, involving a victim and offender known to one another, usually sharing an emotional attachment and experiencing a fatal conflict arising out of that attachment. It seems that the closest prison analog to such emotional attachment is homosexuality.

This being the case, the various patterns of homosexuality in prison ought to be studied far more extensively than they have been, but with specific attention to the potential for violence inherent in such patterns. This would include patterns of seduction, exploitation, competition and protection. It should also be concerned with the extent of passive or active complicity in inmate homosexuality by prison staff. Such research might produce recommendations for augmented surveillance and control of homosexuality in prison, given its apparent relation to homicide.

The other type of prison homicide—multiple-assailant homicide—deserves far greater study in itself for several reasons. First of all, it appears to be a far more rational and premeditated type of homicide. Connected to the enforcement of prisoner norms, it is more like homicides outside the prison which are planned killings for elimination. These would include the classic underworld "hit" but would also encompass those upperworld homicides whose existence and extent are often suspected but seldom proved and, which likewise involve the rational elimination of another human being: the realm of "secret" homicide—certain fatal automobile and hunting "accidents." In prison, it seems to be a violent solution—an

Endlosung—by violent men, in a place where inhabitants are daily surrounded by violence.

But even more interesting is the observation that, over and above whatever causes for homicidal violence are inherent in the prisoner community, the homicides which we have called "multiple-assailant homicides" are committed by those singularly experienced in violence. One might recite the usual sociological litany on the effects of the exposure of individuals, both inside and outside of prison, to the "subculture of violence." However, it would seem that the apparent concentration of this type of homicide in a group of offenders with histories of violent behavior argues at least equally well for a more clinical approach to the study of homicide.

Once such a group of offenders was identified, some intensive effort would seem justified to establish medical and psychiatric profiles directed to such areas as genetic anomalies, brain injury, long-term drug and alcohol use, and parental history of disease. Some attempt at this was carried out by the present study, but the only significant finding was that the routinely maintained records which were useful data for other aspects of the study of prison homicide were quite inadequate for this sort of clinical assessment. Records on the medical and psychiatric condition of offenders were either incomplete or superficial.

Since in the large majority of cases of prison homicide victims were killed by weapons (three-quarters of the cases by stabbing or cutting instruments), further research into the weapons culture of prisons would seem fruitful. Though a lethal weapon can be turned out of practically any sort of commonly found material, prison would appear to be a setting where limiting access to such materials would be easiest. How, then, do prisoners obtain or manufacture knives? Where do they conceal them? How effective in discovering them are routine shakedowns? To what degree could increased use of metal detection devices within the prison reduce the possession of knives?

Finally, the seeming ambiguity of the density factor in prison populations in relation to homicides needs to be further studied. If—as it appears—mere density of population does not accurately predict prison homicide, is there some intervening variable which together with density may be a cause of homicide? Recent studies have suggested that overcrowding is not necessarily connected to hostility but may serve to intensify whatever set of social relationships exist in the relevant population. If this is so, then further research is necessary to determine precisely the nature of social relationships in prison whose potential for violence may be heightened by population density.

We have concluded that, in general, individual factors seem to weigh more heavily in the etiology of prison homicide than do environmental factors. However, this should not obscure the obvious fact that personalities and behavioral patterns may have been shaped by the social and physical environment long before the person is incarcerated. In addition, violence in prison may—in part—be a reflection of the forces which induce violence in the larger society. It should also be emphasized that there is nothing in this work which ought to be interpreted as support for the status quo. To find 130 homicides in state and federal prisons in a single year represents a situation which should be of concern to citizens and correctional administrators alike.

This has been a statistical study, and statistics are the jargon of science. But statistics describe an average condition; they do not necessarily speak to the morality of the human condition. To conclude (as we have), for example, that race is not a major factor in prison homicide is to make a normative statement. There are prisons in which racial tensions and attendant violence may be very high. To dismiss these conditions on the basis of this or any similar study is to do a disservice to science and mankind. This document should serve not as a justification for what is, but as a call to further responsibility and action.

CHAPTER 1

Notes

1. There are several problems attendant on the use of this series as an information source. The data are presented in absolute numbers for each year under the broader heading "Departures" in tables on the movement of prisoners. The incidence of mortality in these tables is cross-tabulated by the variables of prison system, sex, deaths by age, race, length of sentence or confinement, type of custody, offense, and cause of death. The absence of such information severely limits the inferences which can be drawn. In addition to these limitations, it should be pointed out that the data are primarily intended for administrative use and thus are not tabulated in a manner conducive to the application of population analysis techniques. Finally, and perhaps most importantly, participation in the National Prisoner Statistics Program is purely voluntary, with the result that there are few positive safeguards on the reliability of the reported information. See National Prisoner Statistics series, *Prisoners in State and Federal Institutions for Adult Felons* (Washington, D.C., 1962-1972).

2. The CDR is simply the quotient of the total number of deaths occurring in a population during a given time interval divided by the number of person-years in the subject population during the same interval, multiplied by one thousand to eliminate unwieldy decimal places. The midyear population, estimated by

summing the population at the beginning and the end of the year and dividing by two, is used in calculating person-years lived. For a more detailed discussion of the CDR and "person-years lived," see George W. Barclay, *Techniques of Population Analysis* (New York, 1958), pp. 34-44, 100-101, 134-136.

3. In 1970, 22.8% of all males were fifty years of age or older. According to the *Statistical Report* of the federal Bureau of Prisons for 1970, only 7.4% of sentenced prisoners confined in Bureau of Prisons institutions were more than forty-nine years of age (*Statistical Report: Fiscal Years 1969 and 1970* [Washington, D.C. 1970]). This difference is important since better than two-thirds of all deaths in the U.S. are among persons fifty or more years of age. Conversely, some 39.5% of all Americans had not yet attained the age of twenty, in contrast to prisons where all but 5.6% of the inmates had reached twenty years of age. Fewer than one-tenth of all deaths in the U.S. occur among persons less than twenty years old.

4. The statistical technique used here is known as indirect standardization. For a full explication of the procedures involved, see Barclay, pp. 161-166. To calculate the number of expected deaths for 1966, age-specific death rates were taken from *Vital Statistics: 1966,* vol. 2 (Public Health Service, Washington, D.C. 1968), multiplied times the appropriate age-race categories for male federal prisoners and the resulting products summed. Since the Federal Bureau of Prisons' *Statistical Report: Fiscal Year 1966* (Washington, D.C. n.d.) did not include an age-sex-race breakdown per se, the distributions for the federal prison population had to be synthesized from three different sources. Age and race breakdowns came from the *Statistical Report,* Table A-6. In the NPS reports for 1966, a table was found (*Prisoners in State and Federal Institutions for Adult Felons,* Washington, D.C. n.d., p. 12) dividing the federal prisoners by sex. Making the assumption that the sexual and racial composition was uniform throughout age structure of the federal population, a white-non-white age distribution for males in federal custody was calculated for the year 1966.

5. Information from the *Statistical Report: Fiscal Years 1969 and 1970* (Washington, D.C. 1970) detailed the age-race breakdown of the sentenced population in federal institutions. Also contained within was a sex-by-race cross-tabulation of federal prisoners under sentence. Making the assumption that females were evenly distributed through the age compositions of both racial groups of prisoners, an age-race composition for sentenced male felons in federal custody was arranged for the year 1969. *Vital Statistics of the United States: 1969,* vol. 2 (Washington, D.C. 1974) was then consulted and age-specific death rates derived for the year 1969 to effect the standardization.

6. Information from the *Statistical Report: Fiscal Year 1973* (Washington, D.C. n.d.) gave a precise race and age breakdown for adult males in the U.S. Bureau of Prisons' institutions having a population exceeding 200. No extraordinary assumptions were required. The number of deaths for these institutions during 1973 was collected during the field research. Data for the general population were obtained from the most recently published volume of *Vital Statistics of the United States: 1971* (Washington, D.C., 1975).

7. Only federal institutions with adult male felon populations in excess of 200 were included. In the next few paragraphs, the word "system" has special connotations. It means the prisons in a state that met the criteria, whether or not the prison had a homicide. It does not include prisons in a state which did not meet our criteria. The figures are not directly comparable for states since staff and inmate deaths are not separated, which inflates the population at risk.

8. Motor vehicle accidents account for slightly fewer than one-half of all accidental deaths among males. Falls are second in frequency, followed by "fire and explosion" and drowning. (Albert P. Iskrant and Paul V. Joliet, *Accidents and Homicide* [Cambridge, Mass., 1968], p. 147.)

CHAPTER 2

Notes

1. The term "staff" includes custodial personnel, administrative personnel, and the residual staff whose functions are noncustodial. In 1973, all but one of the staff who died were custodial personnel. The exception was a cooking instructor.

2. One state in the North Central region did not forward information on its single-homicide event, while another state in this region reported two homicides but sent information on only one event.

3. Three of these firearm deaths were escaping prisoners shot by guards with rifles. In two different incidents at the same institution, inmates were killed by unidentified assailants using handguns. The two remaining gun deaths stemmed from a single incident. Guard hostages had been taken by inmates, including an inmate armed with a small-caliber handgun. This handgun was used to slay a hostage. Later that same afternoon, a police sniper inadvertently shot and killed a second hostage using a .308-caliber rifle with scope.

4. One victim was strangled, stabbed 170 times, stuffed into a garbage can, and finally set afire. Another victim was stabbed 97 times.

5. These categories and their descriptions are as follows: *Homosexual* – if the homicide had been linked to homosexual relations, disputes or jealousies between the participants. *Debts* – if the homicide was related to disputes over money or property other than intoxicants. *Gang* – if the death was tied to power struggles between or within formal gangs of inmates in the prison. *Drugs* – relating to the distribution, possession or sale of intoxicants. *"Snitch"* – if the victim had been seen as an informer by the assailants who sought reprisals. *Race* – if the incident was primarily racial. *Escape* – if the victim was an inmate attempting to escape. *Argument* – if the slaying stemmed from a heated confrontation over considerations not included above. *Fight* – if the homicide was concomitant with a fight, particularly if no other motive was discerned. This category was used when the homicide resulted from a general "free-for-all" in which the victim apparently had not been singled out in advance. The category *Other*

includes all known motives not included above. Among these were a victim who was killed after making fun of his assailant who stuttered, an inmate who was killed by other inmates for "violating" the first hot meal served after the institution had been in an extended period of "lockdown" with cold meals in cells, a guard who was accidentally slain by a police sniper, and an assailant who lashed out at a neutral party because the prison authorities were transferring his "prison wife" to new custody status. Also included here were two guard murders motivated by hatred of guards.

6. The term "white" included Mexican-Americans and Puerto Ricans.

7. It is interesting to note that there is no racial difference with respect to the proportion of cases in which no assailants were identified.

8. There were 130 deaths identified by authorities as being homicides. There may have been more homicides which went undetected for whatever reason. For instance, one state reported no homicides. Based on the size of the institutions in that state, we calculated that the probability of its having no homicides in any of its large institutions was .002. This calculation assumes that events in each institution are independent of one another—which, of course, is not necessarily the case. It is quite possible that homicides were otherwise recorded.

9. The fifty cases where the cause of death was unknown were either ones where the entry on the death certificate was nonspecific (e.g., "multiple stab wounds") or the death certificate was not present.

10. The state police and county sheriff both participated in one investigation. The county sheriff and local police cooperated in another.

CHAPTER 3

Notes

1. The factors bearing on whether or not assailants were identified are many. They include not only whether or not suspected assailants were named, but also considerations of departmental policies, record-keeping practices, and state laws.

2. Subsequent to the analysis, an additional inmate/staff event was uncovered involving a stabbing of a guard by a recalcitrant inmate who refused to leave his cell. The homicide took place on a Friday night in June. The assailant was a kidnapper who had been in the facility for six years.

3. The one homicide reported after the analysis was complete was of a captain with seventeen and a half years' experience.

4. This was the only multiple killing in prison in 1973 other than the event where two other guards were killed, one by an inmate and the other by a police sniper.

Related Readings

Books

Abrahamsen, D. *The Murdering Mind.* New York:Harper & Row, 1973.
_____ *Our Violent Society.* New York:Funk & Wagnalls, 1970.
Adorno, T., et al. *The Authoritarian Personality.* New York:Harper & Row, 1952.
Allen, F. *The Borderland of Criminal Justice: Essays in Law and Criminology.* Chicago:Univ. of Chicago Press, 1964.
Andry, R. *The Short Term Prisoner: A Study in Forensic Psychology.* London: Stevens & Sons, 1963.
Angel, S. *Discouraging Crime Through City Planning.* Berkeley:Univ. of California Press, 1968.
Badillo, H., and M. Haynes. *A Bill of No Rights. Attica and the American Prison System.* New York:Outer Bridge and Lazard, Inc., 1972.
Bandura, A. *Aggression (A Social Learning Analysis).* Santa Cruz, Calif.:Davis Publishing Co., 1973.
Barnes, H. *The Evolution of Penology in Pennsylvania: A Study in American Social History.* Montclair, N.J.:Patterson Smith, 1968.
Barry, J. *Alexander Maconochie of Norfolk Island: A Study of a Pioneer in Penal Reform.* Melbourne, Australia:Oxford Univ. Press, 1958.
Beaumont, G., and A. de Tocqueville. *On the Penitentiary System in the United States and Its Application in France.* Carbondale, Ill.:Southern Ill. Univ. Press, 1964.
Bensing, R., and O. Schroeder. *Homicide in an Urban Community.* Springfield, Ill.: Charles C. Thomas, 1960.

Berkowitz, L. *Aggression: A Social Psychological Analysis.* New York:McGraw-Hill, 1962.

_____*Roots of Aggression: A Re-Examination of the Frustration-Aggression Hypothesis.* New York:Atherton Press, 1969.

Biggs, J. *The Guilty Mind: Psychiatry and the Law of Homicide.* New York:Harcourt Brace Jovanovich, 1955.

Blumenthal, M., et al. *Justifying Violence: Attitudes of American Men.* Ann Arbor, Mich.:Institute for Social Research, 1972.

Bohannan, P., ed. *African Homicide and Suicide.* Princeton, N.J.:Princeton Univ. Press, 1960.

Brearley, H. *Homicide in the United States.* Montclair, N.J.:Patterson Smith, 1969.

Briggs, L. *The Manner of Man That Kills.* Boston:Badger, 1921.

Bromberg, W. *The Mold of Murder: A Psychiatric Study of Homicide.* New York: Grune & Stratton, 1961.

Brophy, J. *The Meaning of Murder.* New York:T.Y. Crowell, 1967.

Buss, A. *The Psychology of Aggression.* New York:John Wiley & Sons, Inc., 1961.

California Criminal Statistics Bureau. *Criminal Homicide in California: A Cohort Study.* Sacramento, 1967.

Campbell, D. *Experimental and Quasi-Experimental Designs for Research.* Chicago: Rand McNally, 1963.

Carroll, L. *Hacks, Blacks and Cons.* Lexington, Mass.:D.C. Heath & Co., 1974.

Carter, L. *The Limits of Order.* Lexington, Mass.:D.C. Heath & Co., 1974.

Carthy, J., and F. Ebling. *The Natural History of Aggression.* New York:Academic Press, 1964.

Cohen, S., and L. Taylor. *Psychological Survival: The Experience of Long-Term Imprisonment.* New York:Random House, 1974.

Cortes, J., and F. Gatti. *Delinquency and Crime.* New York:Academic Press, 1972.

Cressey, D. *The Prison: Studies in Institutional Organization and Change.* New York: Holt, Rinehart & Winston, 1961.

Criminal Justice Commission. *Criminal Homicides in Baltimore, Maryland, 1960-1964.* Baltimore, 1967.

Curtis, L. *Criminal Violence.* Lexington, Mass.:D.C. Heath & Co., 1974.

Dalton, K. *The Premenstrual Syndrome.* Springfield, Ill.:Charles C. Thomas, 1964.

Daniels, D., et al., eds. *Violence and the Struggle for Existence.* Boston:Little, Brown & Co., 1970.

Danto, B. *Jail House Blues.* Orchard Lake, Mich.:Epic Publications, Inc., 1973.

De Renck, A., and R. Porter, eds. *The Mentally Abnormal Offender.* London:J. & A. Churchill Ltd., 1968.

De Silva, H. *Why We Have Automobile Accidents.* New York:John Wiley & Sons, Inc., 1942.

Dollard, J., et al. *Frustration and Aggression.* New Haven, Conn.:Yale Univ. Press, 1939.

Drapkin, I., and E. Viano. *Victimology: A New Focus* (5 vols.). Lexington, Mass.: D.C. Heath & Co., 1974-75.

Duffy, C., and A. Hirshberg. *Sex and Crime.* New York:Doubleday & Co., 1965.

East, W. *Society and the Criminal.* London:H.M.S.O., 1949.

Edelhertz, H., and G. Geis. *Public Compensation to Victims of Crime.* New York: Praeger Pubs., Inc., 1974.

Endleman, S. *Violence in the Streets.* Chicago:Quadrangle Books, 1968.

Esselstyn, T. *The Violent Offender and Corrections.* Washington, D.C.:President's

Commission on Law Enforcement and the Administration of Justice, 1967.

Ferracuti, F., and M. Wolfgang. *Psychological Testing of the Subculture of Violence.* Rome:Bulzoni Editore, 1973.

Fox, R. *The Extra Y Chromosome and Deviant Behavior: A Bibliography.* Toronto: Univ. of Toronto, 1970.

Fox, V. *Violence Behind Bars.* Westport, Conn.:Greenwood Press, 1975.

Freeman, L. *Children Who Kill.* New York:Berkley Publishing Corp., 1962.

Fried, W., and J. Smith. *The Uses of the American Prison.* Lexington, Mass.:D.C. Heath & Co., 1974.

Gellhorn, E. *Biological Foundation of Emotion.* Glenview, Ill.:Scott, Foresman and Co., 1968.

Glaser, D. *Crime in the City.* New York:Harper & Row, 1970.

_____et al. *The Violent Offender.* Washington, D.C.:U.S. Government Printing Office, 1966.

Glover, E. *The Roots of Crime.* London:International Universities Press, 1960.

Goldfarb, R. *Jails: The Ultimate Ghetto.* New York:Doubleday & Co., Inc., 1975.

Goldstein, L. *Research on Human Variables in Safe Motor Vehicle Operation: A Correlational Summary of Predictor Variables and Criterion Measures.* Washington, D.C.:United States Government Printing Office, 1961.

Graham, H., ed. *Violence.* Baltimore:Johns Hopkins Univ. Press, 1971.

Grunhut, M. *Penal Reform: A Comparative Study.* Montclair, N.J.:Patterson Smith, 1972.

Gunn, J. *Violence.* New York:Praeger Pubs., Inc., 1973.

Guttmacher, M. *The Mind of the Murderer.* New York:Farrar, Strauss, & Cudahy, 1960.

Hall, E. *The Hidden Dimension.* Garden City, N.Y.:Doubleday & Co., Inc., 1966.

Halleck, S. *The Politics of Therapy.* New York:Harper & Row, 1971.

_____*Psychiatry and the Dilemmas of Crime.* New York:Harper & Row, 1967.

_____and W. Bromberg. *Psychiatric Aspects of Criminology.* Springfield, Ill.: Charles C. Thomas, 1968.

Harris, R. *Outline of Death Investigation.* Santa Cruz, Calif.:Davis Publishing Co., 1973.

Hartogs, R., and E. Artzt. *Violence: Causes and Solutions.* New York:Dell Pub. Co., Inc., 1970.

Harvard, J. *The Detection of Secret Homicide.* London:Macmillan, 1960.

Henry, A., and J. Short. *Suicide and Homicide.* Glencoe, Ill.:Free Press, 1954.

Hentig, H. von. *The Criminal and His Victim.* New Haven, Conn.:Yale Univ. Press, 1948.

Hibbert, C. *The Roots of Evil.* Boston:Little, Brown and Co., 1963.

Hirschi, T. *Cause of Delinquency.* Los Angeles:Univ. of California Press, 1969.

Hoffman, F. *The Homicide Problem.* Newark, N.J.:The Prudential Press, 1925.

Howard, D. *The English Prisons: Their Past and Their Future.* London:Methuen, 1960.

Irvine, L., and T. Brelje. *Law, Psychiatry and the Mentally Disordered Offender* (2 vols.). Springfield, Ill.:Charles C. Thomas, 1972-73.

Iskrant, A., and P. Joliet. *Accidents and Homicide.* Cambridge, Mass.:Harvard Univ. Press, 1968.

Jeffery, C. *Criminal Responsibility and Mental Disease.* Springfield, Ill.:Charles C. Thomas, 1967.

Johnson, R. *Aggression in Man and Animals.* Philadelphia:W.B. Saunders Co., 1972.

Johnston, N. *The Human Cage: A Brief History of Prison Architecture.* New York: Walker & Co., 1973.

Justice, B. *Violence in the City.* Fort Worth, Tex.:Texas Christian Univ. Press, 1969.

Kerper, H. *Legal Rights of the Convicted.* St. Paul, Minn.:West Publishing Co., 1974.

Knutson, J. *The Control of Aggression.* Chicago:Aldine Publishing Co., 1973.

Krantz, S. *The Law of Corrections and Prisoners' Rights.* St. Paul, Minn.:West Publishing Co., 1973.

Langbert, R. *Homicide in the United States, 1950-1964.* Washington, D.C.:U.S. Government Printing Office, 1967.

Lawes, L. *Meet the Murderer.* New York:Harper & Row, 1940.

Lion, J. *Evaluation and Management of the Violent Patient.* Springfield, Ill.:Charles C. Thomas, 1972.

Lorenz, K. *On Aggression.* New York:Harcourt Brace & World, 1966.

MacDonald, J. *Homicidal Threats.* Springfield, Ill.:Charles C. Thomas, 1968.

———*The Murderer and His Victim.* Springfield, Ill.:Charles C. Thomas, 1961.

———*Psychiatry and the Criminal.* Springfield, Ill.:Charles C. Thomas, 1969.

———et al. *Human Variables in Motor Vehicle Accidents: A Review of the Literature.* Boston:Harvard School of Public Health, 1955.

McLintock, F. *Crimes of Violence.* Cambridge, England:Cambridge Univ., 1963.

MacMahon, B., et al. *Epidemiologic Methods.* Boston, Little, Brown, & Co., 1960.

Mannheim, H. *Comparative Criminology.* Boston:Houghton Mifflin Co., 1965.

Maple, T., and D. Matheson. *Aggression, Hostility and Violence.* New York:Holt, Rinehart & Winston, 1973.

Mark, V., and F. Erwin. *Violence and the Brain.* New York:Harper & Row, 1970.

Morland, H. *Pattern of Murder.* London:Elek Book Ltd., 1966.

Morris, A. *Homicide: An Approach to the Problem of Crime.* Boston:Boston Univ. Press, 1955.

Morris, N., and G. Hawkins. *The Honest Politician's Guide to Crime Control.* Chicago: 1969.

Morris, T. *The Criminal Area.* London:Routledge & Kegan Paul, 1957.

———and L. Blom-Cooper. *A Calendar of Murder: Criminal Homicide in England since 1957.* London:M. Joseph, 1964.

———et al. *Pentonville: A Sociological Study of an English Prison.* London: Routledge & Kegan Paul, 1963.

Mosley, A. *Research of Fatal Highway Collisions.* Boston:Harvard Medical School, 1963.

Mowat, R. *Morbid Jealousy and Murder.* London:Tavistock Publications, 1966.

Moyer, K. *The Physiology of Hostility.* Chicago:Markham, 1971.

Moynihan, D. *Violent Crime: The Challenge to Our Cities.* New York:George Braziller, 1969.

Mulvihill, D., et al. *Crimes of Violence* (3 vols.). Washington, D.C.:U.S. Government Printing Office, 1969.

Ohio Bureau of Juvenile Research. *A Group Study of Juvenile Homicide.* Columbus, Ohio, 1949.

Oughton, F. *Murder Investigation.* London:Elek Books, 1971.

Palmer, S. *The Psychology of Murder.* New York:Thomas Y. Crowell, 1960.

———*A Study of Murder.* New York:Thomas Y. Crowell, 1960.

———*The Violent Society.* New Haven, Conn.:College and University Press, 1972.

Panagopoulos, L., and C. Miller. *An Analysis of Recidivism among Convicted Murderers.* Boston:Massachusetts Department of Correction, 1970.

Parry, M. *Aggression on the Road.* London:Tavistock, 1968.

Pugh, R. *Imprisonment in Medieval England.* London:Cambridge Univ. Press, 1968.

Rappeport, J. *The Clinical Evaluation of the Dangerousness of the Mentally Ill.* Springfield, Ill.:Charles C. Thomas, 1967.

Ray, I. *Treatise on the Medical Jurisprudence of Insanity* (5th ed.). New York: Arno Press, 1975.

Reinhardt, J. *Nothing Left but Murder.* Lincoln, Neb.:Johnson Publishing Co.. 1970.

———*The Psychology of Strange Killers.* Springfield, Ill.:Charles C. Thomas, 1962.

Richardson, L. *Statistics of Deadly Quarrels.* Pittsburgh:Boxwood Press, 1960.

Roberts, R. *Alcohol Safety Study. The Social Ecology of Violent Death in a Metropolitan Community. A Comparison of Traffic Fatalities and Other Causes of Death.* Washington, D.C.:U.S. Government Printing Office, 1968.

Robins, L. *Deviant Children Grown Up.* Baltimore:Williams & Wilkins, 1968.

Roebuck, J. *Criminal Typology.* Springfield, Ill.:Charles C. Thomas, 1967.

Rose, T. *Violence in America.* New York:Random House, 1970.

Royal Commission on Capital Punishment. 1949-1953 Report. London:H.M.S.O., 1953.

Rubin, S. *The Law of Criminal Correction.* St. Paul, Minn.:West Publishing Co.. 1973.

Sanford, N., and C. Comstock. *Sanctions for Evil.* San Francisco:Jossey-Bass. Inc., 1971.

Schachter, S. *Emotion, Obesity and Crime.* New York:Academic Press, 1971.

Schafer, S. *The Victim and His Criminal.* New York:Random House, 1968.

Scherer, K., et al. *Human Aggression and Conflict.* Englewood Cliffs, N.J.:Prentice Hall,

Schoenfeld, C. *Psychoanalysis and the Law.* Springfield, Ill.:Charles C. Thomas, 1973.

Schumacher, M. *Violent Offending: A Report on Recent Trends in Violent Offending and Some Characteristics of the Violent Offender.* Wellington, N.Z.:Dept. of Justice, New Zealand, 1971.

Scott, J. *Aggression.* Chicago:Univ. of Chicago Press, 1958.

Sellin, T. *Capital Punishment.* New York:Harper & Row, 1967.

———and M. Wolfgang. *The Measurement of Delinquency.* Montclair, N.J.: Patterson Smith, 1975.

Shagass, C., and J. Zubin. *Neurobiological Aspects of Psychopathology.* New York, Grune & Stratton, Inc. 1969.

Shah, S. *Report on the XYY Chromosomal Abnormality.* Washington, D.C.:U.S. Government Printing Office, 1970.

Shaw, L., and H. Sichel. *Accident Proneness.* New York:Pergamon Press, 1971.

Sherrill, R. *The Saturday Night Special.* New York:Charterhouse, 1973.

Silving, H. *Mental Incapacity and Criminal Conduct.* Springfield, Ill.:Charles C. Thomas, 1967.

Singer, J. *The Control of Aggression and Violence.* New York:Academic Press, 1971.

Slovenko, R. *Sexual Behavior and the Law.* Springfield, Ill.:Charles C. Thomas, 1965.

Snyder, G. *Motor Manslaughter.* Toronto:Univ. of Toronto, 1937.

Snyder, L. *Homicide Investigation.* Santa Cruz, Calif.:Davis Publishing Co., 1973.
Sommer, R. *Personal Space.* Englewood Cliffs, N.J.:Prentice-Hall, 1969.
Spitz, W., and R. Fisher. *Medicolegal Investigation of Death.* Santa Cruz, Calif.: Davis Publishing Co., 1973.
Storr, A. *Human Aggression.* New York:Atheneum, 1968.
Sturup, G. *Treating the "Untreatable" Chronic Criminals at Herstedvester.* Baltimore: Johns Hopkins Univ. Press, 1968.
Szasz, T. *Psychiatric Justice.* New York:Macmillan, 1965.
Tabachnick, N. *Accident or Suicide?* Springfield, Ill.:Charles C. Thomas, 1973.
Toch, H. *Violent Men.* Chicago:Aldine, 1969.
Valentine, G. *Chromosome Disorders.* (2nd ed.) New York:Lippincott, 1970.
Verkko, V. *Homicides and Suicides in Finland and Their Dependence on National Character.* Copenhagen:G.E.C. Gads Forlag, 1951.
Walker, N. *Crime and Insanity in England.* Edinburgh:Edinburgh Univ. Press, 1968.
Walls, H. *Forensic Science.* New York:Praeger Pubs, Inc., 1974.
Watson, A. *Medico-Legal Treatise on Homicide by External Violence, in Relation to the Causes of Death by Violence, etc.* Edinburgh:MacLachlan, Stewart & Co., 1842.
Wertham, F. *The Show of Violence.* New York:Greenwood Press, 1949.
_____*A Sign for Cain.* New York:Macmillan, 1966.
West, D. *Criminological Implications of Chromosome Abnormalities.* Cambridge, England:Cambridge Univ., 1969.
_____*The Habitual Prisoner: An Enquiry by the Cambridge Institute of Criminology.* Cambridge, England:Cambridge Univ., 1963.
_____*Murder Followed by Suicide.* Cambridge:Harvard Univ. Press, 1966.
_____*Research on Violence.* Cambridge, England:Cambridge Univ., 1974.
Whitlock, F. *Death on the Road.* London:Tavistock, 1971.
Wilkins, L. *Evaluation of Penal Measures.* New York:Random House, 1969.
Willett, T. *Criminal on the Road.* London:Tavistock, 1964.
Wolfgang, M. *Patterns in Criminal Homicide.* Philadelphia:Univ. of Pennsylvania Press, 1958.
_____*Studies in Homicide.* New York:Harper & Row, 1967.
_____*Violent Behavior.* Cambridge, England:W. Heffer & Sons, Ltd., 1969.
_____and F. Ferracuti. *The Subculture of Violence.* New York:Barnes & Noble, 1967.
Yablonsky, L. *The Violent Gang.* New York:Penguin Books, 1962.
Zilboorg, G. *The Psychology of the Criminal Act and Punishment.* New York:Greenwood Press, 1954.

Articles

Abdullah, S., et al. "Extra Y chromosome and its psychiatric implications." *Archives of General Psychiatry,* 21(1969), 497-501.
Abrahamsen, D. "Psychiatric aspects of delinquency." *Journal of Educational Sociology,* 24(1950), 40-44.
_____"Study of 102 sex offenders at Sing Sing." *Federal Probation,* 14(1950), 26-32.
_____"A study of Lee Harvey Oswald: psychological capability of murder." *New York Academy Medical Bulletin,* 43(1967), 861-888.

Adams, M. "Age and crime, medical and sociologic characteristics of prisoners over 50." *Geriatrics,* 16(1961), 177-181.

Adelson, L. "Slaughter of the innocents: a study of forty-six homicides in which the victims were children." *New England Journal of Medicine,* 6(1961), 1345-1349.

————. "Some medicolegal observations on infanticide." *Journal of Forensic Sciences,* 4(1959), 60-72.

Akman, D. "Homicides and assaults in Canadian penitentiaries." *Canadian Journal of Corrections,* 8(1966), 284-299.

Albert, R. "The role of mass media and the effect of aggressive film content upon children's aggressive responses and identification choices." *Genetic Psychological Monographs,* 55(1957), 221-285.

Alderton, H., and B. Hoddinott. "A controlled study of the use of thioridazine in the treatment of hyperactive and aggressive children in a children's psychiatric Hospital." *Canadian Psychiatric Association Journal,* 9(1964), 239-247.

Allen, H., et al. "The social and bio-medical correlates of sociopathy." *Criminologica,* 6(1968-1969), 68-75.

Allen, M. "A cross cultural study of aggression and crime." *Journal of Cross-Cultural Psychology,* 3(1972), 259-271.

Allen, T. "Patterns of escape and self-destructive behavior in a correctional institution." *Correction Psychiatry and Journal of Social Therapy,* 15(1969) 50-58.

Alpers, B. "Personality and emotional disorders associated with hypothalmic lesions." *Association for Research in Nervous Mental Diseases* (1940), 725-748.

Amir, M. "Chromosomal deviation and crime." *Federal Probation,* 34(1970), 55-62.

"An analysis of homicide-suicide." *Journal of Clinical and Experimental Psychopathology,* 19(1939).

Ancel, M. "Principal aspects of modern European penology." *Proceedings of the American Philosophical Society,* 118(1974), 254-259.

Andrade, O. "The criminogenic action of cannabis (marijuana) and narcotics." *Bulletin on Narcotics,* 16(1964), 23-28.

Ansbacher, H. "Lee Harvey Oswald, an Adlerian interpretation." *Psych. Rev.,* 58 (1966), 55-68.

Asaka, A., et al. "XYZ individual in Japanese juvenile delinquents." *Lancet* (1971) 985.

Ashworth, A. "A short note on the English murder rate." *Criminal Law Review,* 15(1969), 645-654.

————. "Self indulged provocation and the homicide set." *Criminal Law Review,* 19(1973), 483-492.

Astin, A. "A factor study of the MMPI psychopathic deviate scale." *Journal of Consulting and Clinical Psychology,* 23(1959), 550-554.

Asuni, T. "Homicide in western Nigeria." *British Journal of Psychiatry,* 115/527, 1105-1113.

Azrin, N., et al. "Extinction induced aggression." *Journal of the Experimental Analysis of Behavior,* 9(1966), 191-204.

————et al. "The opportunity for aggression as an operant reinforcer during aversive stimulation." *Journal of the Experimental Analysis of Behavior,* 8(1965) 171.

Bach-Y-Rita, G. "Episodic dyscontrol, a study of 130 violent patients." *American Journal of Psychiatry,* 127(1971), 49-54.

Bain, R. "The concept of sociopathy." *Sociology and Social Research,* 38(1953), 3-6.

Bak, R. "The schizophrenic defense against aggression." *International Journal of Psychoanalysis,* 35(1954), 129.

Baker, B. "XYY chromosome syndrome and the law." *Criminologica,* 7(1970), 2-35.

Baker, D. "Chromosome errors in men with antisocial behavior: comparison of selected men with Klinefelter's syndrome and XYY chromosome pattern." *Journal of the American Medical Association,* 11(1970), 869-878.

Baker, J. "Indians, alcohol and homicide." *Journal of Social Therapy,* 5(1959), 270-275.

Baker, S. "Tattoos, alcohol and violent death." *Journal of Forensic Sciences,* 16 (1971), 219-225.

Bakwin, H. "Homicidal deaths in infants and children." *Journal of Pediatrics,* 57 (1960), 568-570.

Banay, R. "Conversation with a mass murderer." Journal of Social Therapy, 2(1956), 85-92.

_____"Criminal genesis and the degrees of responsibility in epilepsies." *American Journal of Psychiatry,* 117(1960), 873-876.

_____"Homicide among children." *Federal Probation,* 11(1947), 11-19.

_____"Psychology of a mass murderer." *Journal of Forensic Science,* 1(1956), 1-6.

_____"Study in murder." *Annals of the American Academy of Political and Social Sciences,* 284(1952), 26-32.

_____"A study of 22 men convicted of murder in the first degree." *Journal of Criminal Law and Criminology,* 34(1943), 106-111.

Banghan, J. "Ascertainment of seven YY males in a private neurology practice." *Journal of American Medical Association,* 222(1972), 446-448.

_____"MMPI correlates of prisoner's ideal-self." *Correctional Psychologist,* 5(1972), 194-199.

Banitt, X., et al. "The situational aspects of violence—a research model." *Israel Studies in Criminology,* 1(1970), 241-258.

Banks, C. "Violence." *Howard Journal of Penology and Crime Prevention,* 11(1962), 13-25.

Barclay, A., and R. Haber. "The relation of aggressive to sexual motivation." *Journal of Personality,* 3(1965), 462-475.

Barnhart, K. "A study of homicide in the United States." *Social Science,* 7(1932), 141-159.

Barocas, R. "Some problems in the conception of sociopathy." *Psychiatric Quarterly,* 44(1970), 674-686.

Barter, J. "Crime and LSD: the insanity plea." *American Journal of Psychiatry,* 126(1969), 531-537.

Bartholomew, A. "Alcoholism, drug dependency and sex chromosome abnormalities." *Medical Journal of Australia,* 56(1969), 440-443.

_____"Chromosome survey of persons charged with murder." *Australian and New Zealand Journal of Criminology,* 6(1973), 251-253.

_____and G. Sutherland. "A defense of insanity and the extra Y chromosome." *Australian and New Zealand Journal of Criminology,* 2(1969), 29-37.

Bass, U., et al. "The use of heroin by an offender population—a report over time." *Corrective Psychiatry and Journal of Social Therapy,* 18(1972), 24-30.

Batt, J. "Homicidal incidence in the depressive psychoses." *Journal of Mental Science,* 94(1948), 782-792.

Baumiller, R. "XYZ chromosome genetics." *Social Problems,* 14(1969), 411-418.

Beamish, J., and J. Malfetti. "A psychological comparison of violator and non-violator automobile drivers in the 16 to 19 year age group." *Traffic Safety Research Review* (1962), 12-19.

Bean, F., and R. Cushing. "Criminal homicide punishment and deterrence: methodological and substantive reconsiderations." *Social Science Quarterly*, 52(1971), 521-533.

Beattie, R., and J. Kenney. "Aggressive crimes." *Annals of the American Academy of Political and Social Science*, 364(1966), 73-85.

Beeman, E. "The effect of male hormone on aggressive behaviour in mice." *Physiological Zoology*, 20(1947), 373-405.

Beit-Hallahmi, B. "Motivation for murder: the case of G." *Correctional Psychiatry and Journal of Social Therapy*, 17(1971), 25-30.

_____ "Sexual and aggressive fantasies in violent and non-violent prison inmates." *J. Pers. Ass.*, 35(1971), 326-330.

Belle, O. "The criminal consequences of impotence." *Correctional Psychiatry and Journal of Social Therapy*, 15(1969), 24-27.

Bender, L. "Psychiatric mechanisms in child murderers." *Journal of Nervous and Mental Disease*, 80(1934), 32-47.

Benezech, M. "Somatic, psychiatric and hormonal findings and testicular histology in six XYY psychopaths." *Information Psychiatrique*, 48(1972), 175-193.

Bennett, T., and D. Bennett. "Miranda in prisons: the dilemma of prison discipline and intramural crime." *Buffalo Law Review*, 21(1972), 759-773.

Bensing, R., et al. "Some legal, economic, and social aspects of homicide in an urban area." *Journal of Forensic Science*, 84(1960), 87-99.

Berg, I., and V. Fox. "Factors in homicides committed by 200 males." *The Journal of Social Psychology*, 26(1947), 109-119.

Berg, J., et al. "Sex chromation survey of women in a special psychiatric hospital." *Nature*, 222(1969), 896-897.

Berkowitz, L. "The concept of aggressive drive: some additional considerations." L. Berkowitz, ed., *Advances in Experimental Social Psychology* (New York, 1965), Vol. 2.

_____ "The contagion of violence, an S–R mediational analysis of some effects of observed aggression." *Nebraska Symposium on Motivation*, 18(1970), 95-135.

_____ "Experiments on automatism and intent in human aggression," C. Clemente and D. Lindsley, eds., *Aggression and Defense; Neural Mechanisms and Social Patterns* (Los Angeles, 1967), 243-266.

_____ "Frustrations, comparisons and other sources of emotion arousal as contributors to social unrest." *Journal of Social Issues*, 28(1972), 77-91.

_____ "The study of urban violence: some implications of laboratory studies of frustration and aggression," L. Masotti and D. Bowen, eds., *Riots and Rebellion* (Beverly Hills, Calif., 1968).

_____ and A. Le Page. "Weapons as aggression-eliciting stimuli." *Journal of Personality and Social Psychology*, 7(1967), 202-207.

Bernard, V., et al. "Dehumanization," N. Sanford and C. Comstock, eds., *Sanctions for Evil* (San Francisco, 1971).

Berne, E. "Cultural aspects of a multiple murder." *Psychiatric Quarterly Supplement*, 24(1950), 250-269.

Bery, I., and V. Fox. "Factors in homicides committed by 200 males.' *Journal of Social Psychology*, 26(1947), 109-119.

Bettelheim, B. "Violence. A neglected mode of behavior." *Annals of the American*

Academy of Political and Social Sciences, 364(1966), 50-59.

Betts, G. "The detection of incipient army criminals." *Science,* 106(1947), 93-106.

Blackburn, R. "MMPI dimensions of sociability and impulse control." *Journal of Consulting and Clinical Psychology,* 37(1971), 166.

_____ "Personality types among abnormal homicides." *British Journal of Criminology,* 11(1971), 14-31.

Blackman, N. "Sudden murder: three clues to preventive interaction." *Archives of General Psychiatry,* 8(1963), 289-294.

Block, R., and F. Zimring. "Homicide in Chicago, 1965-1970." *Journal of Research in Crime and Delinquency,* 10(1973), 1-12.

Blom-Cooper, L. "Preventable homicide." *Howard Journal of Penology and Crime Prevention,* 11(1965), 297-308.

Blum, R. "Mind-altering drugs and dangerous behavior: alcohol," President's Commission on Law Enforcement and the Administration of Justice, *Task Force Report: Drunkenness* (Washington, 1967).

_____ "Mind-altering drugs and dangerous behavior: dangerous drugs," President's Commission on Law Enforcement and the Administration of Justice, *Task Force Report: Narcotics and Drug Abuse* (Washington, 1967).

_____ "Mind-altering drugs and dangerous behavior: narcotics," President's Commission on Law Enforcement and the Administration of Justice, *Task Force Report: Narcotics and Drug Abuse* (Washington, 1967).

Boelkins, R., and J. Heiser. "Biological bases of aggression," D. Daniels et al., *Violence and the Struggle for Existence* (Boston, 1970).

Bourdouris, J. "Homicide and the family." *Journal of Marriage and the Family,* 33(1971), 667-676.

Bowen, D. "Homicide at sea." *Medicine, Science and the Law,* 12(1972), 185-187.

Brearley, H. "The Negro and Homicide." *Social Forces,* 9(1930), 247-253.

Breslau, N. "XYY health and law." *Southern Medical Journal,* 63(1970), 831-836.

Brewer, C. "Murder and the McNaughten Rules: the importance of adequate medical examination." *Australian and New Zealand Journal of Criminology,* 4(1971), 941-1000.

Brittain, R. "The sadistic murderer." *Medicine, Science and the Law,* 10(1970), 198-207.

Brown, B., and J. Spevacek. "Disciplinary offenses and offenders at two differing correctional institutions." *Correctional Psychiatry and Journal of Social Therapy,* 17(1971), 48-56.

Brown, R. "Historical patterns of violence in America." H. Graham and T. Gurr, *The History of Violence in America* (New York, 1969).

Buki, R. "The use of psychotropic drugs in the rehabilitation of sex-deviated criminals." *American Journal of Psychiatry,* 120(1964), 1170-1175.

Bullock, H. "Urban homicide in theory and fact." *Journal of Criminal Law, Criminology and Police Science,* 45(1955), 565-575.

Burke, K. "The XYY syndrome, genetics behavior and the law." *Denver Law Journal,* 46(1969), 261-284.

Burnand, G. et al. "Some psychological test characteristics of Klinefelter's syndrome." *British Journal of Psychiatry,* 113(1967), 1091-1096.

Burt, R. "Biotechnology and anti-social conduct: controlling the controllers." *Ohio State Law Forum Lectures* (1974).

Butler, J. "Diagnostic significance of the tattoo in psychotic homicide." *Correctional Psychiatry and Journal of Social Therapy,* 14(1968), 110-113.

Bychowski, G. "Dynamics and predictability of dangerous psychotic behavior," J. Rappeport, ed., *The Clinical Evaluation of the Dangerousness of the Mentally Ill* (Springfield, Ill. 1967).

Calhoun, J. "Population density and social pathology." *Scientific American,* 206 (1962), 139-146.

Cameron, J., et al. "The battered child syndrome." *Medicine, Science and the Law,* 6(1966), 1-21.

Cardarelli, A. "An analysis of police killed by criminal action: 1961-63." *Journal of Criminal Law, Criminology, and Police Science,* 59(1968), 447-453.

Carr-Hill, R. "Victims of our typologies,"   Oxford University Penal Research Unit, *The Violent Offender—Reality or Illusion?* (Oxford, 1970).

Carroll, J., and G. Fuller. "An MMPI comparison of three groups of criminals." *Journal of Clinical Psychology,* 27(1971), 240-242.

Carstairs, G. "Overcrowding and human aggression." H. Graham and T. Gurr, *The History of Violence in America* (New York, 1969).

Casey, M., et al. "XY chromosomes and antisocial behavior." *Lancet* (1966), 11-13.

Cason, H. "A statistical study of 500 psychopathic prisoners." *Pescor Medical Journal,* 61(1946), 557-574.

Cassidy, J. "Personality study of 200 murderers."*Journal of Criminal Psychopathology,* 2(1941), 296-304.

Cevbus, G. "Seasonal variation in some mental health statistics, suicides, homicides, psychiatric admissions and institution placement of the retarded." *Journal of Clinical Psychology,* 26(1970), 61-63.

Christensen, A. "Psychological studies of ten patients with the XYY syndrome." *British Journal of Psychiatry,* 123(1973), 219-221.

Christie, T. "The manic-depressive psychoses in relation to crime." *Medico-Legal Journal,* 10(1942), 10-21.

Claghorn, J. "Self mutilation in a prison mental hospital." *Corrective Psychiatry and Journal of Social Therapy,* 13(1967), 133-141.

Clapham, B.   "An interesting case of hypoglycaemia." *Medico-Legal Journal,* 33(1965), 72-73.

Clark, G. "Sex chromosomes, crime and psychosis." *American Journal of Psychiatry,* 126(1970), 1659-1663.

Clark, J. "The relationship between MMPI scores and psychiatric classification of army general prisoners." *Journal of Clinical Psychopathology,* 8(1957), 86-89.

Cleveland, F. "Homicidal poisoning." *Temple Law Quarterly,* 31(1958), 323-329.
_____ "Problem in homicide investigation IV: the relationship of alcohol to homicide." *Cincinnati Journal of Medicine,* 36(1955), 28-30.

Cleveland, W. "Radioulnar synostosis behavioral disturbance and XYY chromosomes." *Journal of Pediatrics,* 74(1966), 103-106.

Climent, C. "Historical data in the evaluation of violent subjects. A hypothesis-generating study." *Archives of General Psychiatry,* 27(1972), 621-624.

Cline, V. "Life history correlates of delinquent and psychopathic behavior." *Journal of Clinical Psychology,* 15(1959), 266-270.

Cloninger, C. "The role of sociopathy and hysteria in the antisocial woman." *American Journal of Psychiatry,* 23(1970), 554-558.

Cohen, J. "The geography of crime." *The Annals of the American Academy of Political and Social Science,* 217(1941), 29-37.

Cohen, L. "The pattern of murder in insanity: a criterion of the murderer's abnormality." *Journal of Criminal Law, Criminology, and Police Science,* 37(1946), 262-287.

_____ and H. Freeman. "How dangerous to the community are state hospital patients?" *Connecticut Medical Journal,* 9(1945), 697-700.

Conger, J., et al. "Psychological and psycho-physiological factors in motor vehicle accidents." *Journal of the American Medical Association,* 169(1959), 1581-1587.

Conner, R., and S. Levine. "Hormonal influences on aggressive behaviour," S. Garattini and E. Siggs, eds., *Aggressive Behaviour* (New York, 1969).

Connor, W. "Criminal homicide, U.S.S.R./U.S.A.: reflections on Soviet data in a comparative framework." *Journal of Criminal Law, Criminology, and Police Science,* 64(1973), 111-117.

Conrad, J. "Violence in prison." *Annals of the American Academy of Political and Social Science,* 363(1966), 113-119.

Cook, S. "Criminal behavior and the use of beverage alcohol." *Canadian Journal of Corrections,* 4(1962), 83-102.

Coppen, A., and N. Kessel. "Menstruation and personality." *British Journal of Psychiatry,* 109(1963), 711-721.

Cormier, B. "Depression and persistent criminality." *Canadian Psychiatric Association Journal,* 2(1966), S-208-220.

_____ "Violence—individual and collective aspects." *Criminology,* 9(1971), 99-116.

_____ et al. "The psychodynamics of homicide committed in a specific relationship." *Canadian Journal of Criminology and Corrections,* 13(1971), 1-8.

Corsini, R. "Appearance and criminality." *American Journal of Sociology,* 65(1959), 49-51.

Couleter, W. "The Szondi Test and the prediction of antisocial behavior." *Journal of Projective Techniques,* 23(1959), 24-29.

Cruvant, B. "The murderer in the mental institution." *Annals of the American Academy of Political and Social Science,* 284(1952), 35-44.

Curtis, G. "Etiological factors in first-degree murder." *Journal of the American Medical Association,* 168(1958), 1755-1758.

Daimer, D. "The gang subculture in an institution." *California Youth Authority Quarterly,* 26(1973), 13-19.

Dalton, K. "Menstruation and accidents." *Accident Research: Methods and Approaches* (New York, 1964).

Daly, R. "Mental illness and patterns of behavior in 10 XYY males." *Journal of Nervous Mental Disorders,* 149(1969), 318-327.

Danto, B. "Firearms and their role in homicide and suicide." *Life-Threatening Behavior,* Vol. 1, (1971).

Davenport, J. "Comment: 20 years of homicide in Texas." *Texas Law Review,* 25(1957), 634-640.

Davis, P. "Three thyrotoxic criminals." *Ann. Int. Med.,* 74(1971), 743-745.

Davis, R. "XYY and crime." *Lancet* (1970), 7682.

_____ et al. "XYY and crime." *Lancet* (1970), 1086.

De Bault, L. "Incidence of XYY and XXY individuals in a security hospital population." *Diseases of the Nervous System,* 33(1972), 590-593.

De Leon,.·C. "Threatened homicide—a medical emergency." *Journal of the National Medical Association,* 53(1961), 467-472.

Delgado, J. "Aggression and defense under cerebral radio control." O. Clemente and D. Lindsley, eds., *Aggression and Defense* (Berkeley, Calif. 1967).

De Porte, J., and E. Pankhurst. "Homicide in New York State. A statistical study of the victims and criminals in 37 counties in 1921-30." *Human Biology,* 7(1935), 47-73.

Diamond, B. "Identification and the sociopathic personality." *Archives of Criminal Psychodynamics,* 4(1966), 456-465.

Dickey, J. "Culpable homicides in resisting arrest." *Cornell Law Quarterly,* 18(1933), 373-390.

Distefano, M. "Prisoner mood-shifts during initial incarceration." *American Journal of Corrections,* 26(1964), 12-14.

Driver, E. "Interaction and criminal homicide in India." *Social Forces,* 40(1961), 153-158.

Dublin, L., and B. Bunzel. "Thou Shalt Not Kill: a study in homicide in the United States." *Survey Graphic,* 24(1935), 127-131.

Duffy, J. "Search for XYY syndrome in psychiatrically disturbed children and adolescent juvenile delinquents: a preliminary report." *Child Psychiatry and Human Development,* 2(1971), 50-53.

Duncan, G., et al. "Etiological factors in first degree murder," M. Wolfgang, ed., *Studies in Homicide* (New York, 1967).

Duncan, J. "Murder in the family: a study of some homicidal adolescents." *American Journal of Psychiatry,* 127(1971), 1498-1502.

Easson, W., and R. Steinhilber. "Murderous aggression by children and adolescents." *Archives of General Psychiatry,* 4(1961), 27-35.

Eckert, W. "Murder—its many aspects." *Criminologist,* 5(1970), 11-17.

Ehrenreich, G. "Headache, necrophilia, and murder." *Bulletin of the Menninger Clinic,* 24(1960), 273-287.

Eibl-Eibesfeldt, I. "Aggressive behavior and ritualized fighting in animals." J. Masserman, ed., *Violence and War* (New York, 1963).

_____ "Ontogenetic and maturational studies of aggressive behavior," C. Clemente and D. Lindsley, eds., *Aggression and Defense* (Berkeley, Calif., 1967).

Ellenberger, H. "Violence and dangerousness." *Annales Internationales de Criminologie,* 10(1971), 345-352.

_____ "Reflections on the scientific study of prison life." *Annales Internationales de Criminologie,* 10(1971), 367-376.

Ellinwood, E. "Assault and homicide assaulted with amphetamine abuse." *American Journal of Psychiatry,* 127(1971), 1170-1175.

Ellis, E. "Does the trigger pull the finger? An experimental test of weapons as aggression eliciting stimuli." *Sociometry,* 34(1971), 453-465.

Evseeff, G., and E. Wisniewski. "A psychiatric study of a violent mass murderer." *Journal of Forensic Sciences,* 17(1973), 371-376.

Falek, A. "An attempt to identify prisoners with XYY chromosome complement by psychiatric and psychological means." *Journal of Nervous Mental Disorders,* 150(1970), 165-170.

Falk, G. "The influence of season on the crime rate." *Journal of Criminal Law,*

Criminology and Police Science, 43(1952), 199-213.

Farrell, P. "The XYY syndrome in criminal law. An introduction." *St. Johns Law Review,* 44(1969), 217-219.

Fattig, W. "An XYY survey in a Negro prison population." *Journal of Heredity,* 61(1970), 10.

Felipe, N., and R. Sommer. "Invasions of personal space." *Social Problems,* 14(1966), 206-214.

Ferdon, N. "Chromosomal abnormalities and antisocial behavior." *Journal of General Psychology,* 118(1971), 281-292.

Ferentz, E. "Mental deficiency related to crime." *Journal of Criminal Law, Criminology, and Police Science,* 45(1954), 299-307.

Ferracuti, F. "Recent trends in research on violent behavior." *Annales Internationales de Criminologie,* 2(1965), 315-325.

Filippi, R. "Positive carriers of violence among children." *Mental Hygiene,* 55(1971), 157-164.

Finestone, H. "Narcotics and criminality," M. Clinard and R. Quinney, eds., *Criminal Behavior Systems: A Typology* (New York, 1967).

Fink, L. "Psychiatry and the crisis of the prison system." *American Journal of Psychotherapy,* 27(1973), 579-584.

Finkelstein, B. "Offenses with no apparent motive." *Diseases of the Nervous System,* 29(1968), 310-314.

Fisher, D., et al. "Knives as aggression-eliciting stimuli." *Psychological Reports,* 24(1969), 775-760.

Fooner, M. "Victim-induced, victim-invited and victim-precipitated criminality. Some problems in evaluation of proposals for victim compensation." *Issues in Criminology,* 2(1966), 297-304.

Ford, R. "Death by hanging of adolescent and young adult males." *Journal of Forensic Science,* 2(1957), 171-176.

Foss, G. "The influence of androgens on sexuality in women." *Lancet* (1951), 667-669.

Fox, R. "XYY chromosomes and crime." *Australian and New Zealand Journal of Criminology,* 2(1969), 5-19.

⸺ "The XYY offender: a modern myth." *Journal of Criminal Law, Criminology, and Police Science,* 62(1971), 59-73.

Fox, V. "Prison riots in a democratic society." *Police,* 16(1972), 35-41.

⸺ "Why prisoners riot." *Federal Probation,* 35(1971), 9-14.

Frankel, E. "One thousand murderers." *Journal of Criminal Law and Criminology,* 29(1939), 672-688.

Friedrich, V., et al. "Chromosome study in forensic psychiatric patients." *Journal of Legal Medicine,* 68(1971), 138-148.

Frost, B. "The pattern of WISC scores in a group of juvenile sociopaths." *Journal of Clinical Psychology,* 18(1962), 354-355.

Gallemore, J., and J. Panton. "Inmate response to lengthy death row confinement." *American Journal of Psychiatry,* 129(1972), 167-172.

Galliher, J. "Change in a correctional institution; a case study in the tightening-up process." *Crime and Delinquency,* 18(1972), 263-270.

Galvin, J. "Psychiatric study of a mass murderer." *American Journal of Psychology,* 123(1956), 1057-1061.

Garbert, C. "Eskimo infanticide." *Scientific Monthly,* 64(1947), 98-102.

Garfinkel, H. "Research note on inter- and intra-racial homicides." *Social Forces,* 27(1948-49), 369-381.

Garson, G. "The disruption of prison administration: an investigation of alternative theories of the relationship among administrators, reformers, and involuntary social service clients." *Law and Society Review,* 6(1972), 531-561.

———"Force vs. restraint in prison riots." *Crime and Delinquency,* 18(1972), 411-421.

Gastril, R. "Homicide and a regional culture of violence." *American Sociological Review,* 36(1971), 412-427.

Gault, W. "Some remarks on slaughter." *American Journal of Psychology,* 128(1971), 450-454.

Geathner, R., and S. Taylor. "Physical aggression as a function of racial prejudice and the race of the target." *Journal of Personality and Social Psychology,* 27(1973), 207-210.

Geis, G. "Violence in American society." *Current History,* 32(1967), 354-358.

Gendel, E. "Unbalanced chromosomes—unbalanced behavior." *Medical World News,* 77(1969).

Gibbens, T. "Sane and insane homicide." *Journal of Criminal Law, Criminology and Police Science,* 49(1958), 110-115.

———"Alcoholism among prisoners." *Psychological Medicine,* 1(1970), 73-78.

Gibbons, D. "Problems of causal analysis in criminology, a case illustration." *Journal of Research in Crime and Delinquency,* 3(1966), 47-52.

———"Violence in American society—the challenge to corrections." *American Journal of Corrections,* 31(1969), 6-11.

Gibbs, F. "Electroencephalographic study of criminals." *American Journal of Psychology,* 102(1969), 294-304.

Gibson, A. "Early delinquency in relation to broken homes." *Journal of Child Psychology,* 10(1969), 195-204.

Gilbert, M. "The incidence of psychopathy in a group of prisoners referred for psychiatric evaluation." *Archives of Criminal Psychodynamics,* 24(1961), 480-488.

Gill, H. "What is a community prison?" *Federal Probation,* 29(1965), 15-18.

Gillin, J. "Murder as a sociological phenomenon." *Annals of the American Academy of Political and Social Science,* 184(1952), 20-25.

———and F. Ochberg. "Firearms control and violence," D. Daniels et al., eds., *Violence and the Struggle for Existence* (Boston, 1970).

Glaser, D., and J. Stratton. "Measuring inmate change in prison," D. Cressey, ed., *The Prison* (New York, 1961 Holt, Rinehart & Winston).

Gloor, P. "Discussion of brain mechanisms related to aggressive behavior by B. Kaada," C. Clemente and D. Lindsley, eds., *Aggression and Defense: Neural Mechanisms and Social Patterns* (Los Angeles, 1967).

Glueck, S. "Theory and fact in criminology." *British Journal of Delinquency,* 7(1956), 92-109.

Gold, L. "Invitation to homicide." *Journal of Forensic Science,* 10(1965), 415-421.

Gold, M. "Suicide, homicide and the socialization of aggression." *American Journal of Sociology,* 63(1958), 651-661.

Goldin, G. "Violence. The integration of psychiatric and sociological concepts." *Notre Dame Law Review,* 40(1965), 508-516.

Goldman, H. "The simple sociopath; physiologic and sociologic characteristics." *Biol. Psych.,* 3(1971), 77-83.

Goodwin, D. "Alcoholic suicide and homicide." *Quarterly Journal of Studies on Alcohol,* 34(1973), 144-156.

Gordon, J. "The epidemiology of accidents." *American Journal of Public Health,* 39(1949), 504-515.

Green, R., and K. Dalton. "The premenstrual syndrome." *British Medical Journal,* 1(1953), 1007-1014.

Greene, J. "Motivations of a murderer." *Journal of Abnormal Social Psychology,* 43(1948), 526-31.

Greenland, C. "Violence and dangerous behavior associated with mental illness." *International Criminal Police Review,* 27(1972), 190-196.

Gregory, T. "Murder is murder and the guilty can be punished." *ABA Journal,* 32(1946), 544-549.

Grimshaw, A. "Interpreting collective violence as an argument for the importance of social structure." *Annals of the American Academy of Political and Social Science,* 391(1970), 9-20.

Grunhut, M. "Murder and the death penalty in England." *Annals of the American Academy of Political and Social Science,* 284(1952), 158-166.

Gulevich, G., and P. Bourne. "Mental illness and violence," D. Daniels et al., eds., *Violence and the Struggle for Existence* (Boston, 1970).

Gunn, J. "Forensic psychiatry and psychopathic patients." *British Journal of Hospital Medicine,* 5(1971), 260-264.

———"Long-term prisoners." *British Journal of Criminology,* 13(1973), 331-340.

———and G. Fenton. "Epilepsy, automatism, and crime." *Lancet* (1971), 1173-1176.

———and G. Fenton. "Epilepsy in prisons: a diagnostic survey." *British Medical Journal,* 4(1969), 326-329.

Gurvitz, M. "Developments in the concept of psychopathic personality, 1900-1950." *British Journal of Delinquency,* 2(1951), 88-102.

Guttmacher, M. "Diagnosis and etiology of psychopathic personalities." *Proceedings of the American Philosophical Association,* 95(1951), 139.

———"The normal and the sociopathic murderer." M. Wolfgang, ed., *Studies in Homicide* (New York, 1967).

Guze, S., et al. "Criminality and psychiatric disorders." *Archives of General Psychiatry,* 20(1969), 583-591.

Gynther, M. "Critique and notes: crime and psychopathology." *Journal of Abnormal and Social Psychology,* 64(1962), 378-380.

Hakeem, M. "A critique of the psychiatric approach to crime and correction." *Law and Contemporary Problems,* 23(1958), 650-682.

Halleck, S. "Psychopathy freedom and criminal behavior." *Bulletin of the Menninger Clinic,* 30(1966), 128-140.

Hamburger, F. "The penitentiary and paranoia." *Corrective Psychiatry and Journal of Social Therapy,* 13(1967), 225-230.

Handler, J. "Background evidence in murder cases." *Journal of Criminal Law, Criminology, and Police Science,* 51(1960), 317-327.

Hare, R. "Psychopathy, autonomic functioning and the orienting response." *Journal of Abnormal Psychology,* monograph suppl. no. 73(1968).

Harlan, H. "Five hundred homicides." *Journal of Criminal Law and Criminology,* 40(1950), 736-752.

Harlow, H., and G. Griffin. "Induced mental and social deficits in Rhesus monkeys,"

S. Osler and R. Cooke, eds., *The Biological Basis of Mental Retardation* (Baltimore, 1965).

_____and M. Harlow. "Social deprivation in monkeys." *Scientific American,* 207(1962), 137-146.

Hartcollis, P. "Aggressive behavior and the fear of violence." *Adolescence,* 7(1972), 479-490.

Hartman, C. "The key jingler." *Community Mental Health Journal,* 5(1969), 199-205.

Hartmann, D. "Influence of symbolically modeled instrumental aggression and pain cues on aggressive behavior." *Journal of Personality and Social Psychology,* 11(1969), 280-288.

Hawke, C. "Castration and sex crimes." *American Journal of Mental Deficiency,* 55(1950), 220-226.

Hayner, N. "Characteristics of five offender types." *American Sociological Review,* 27(1961), 96-102.

_____"The prison community." *Canadian Journal of Corrections,* 6(1964), 320-324.

Heimburger, R., et al. "Stereotaxic amygdalotomy for epilepsy with aggressive behavior." *Journal of the American Medical Association,* 198(1966), 165-169.

Heller, J. "Human chromosome abnormalities as related to physical and mental dysfunction." *Journal of Heredity,* 60(1969), 239-248.

Heller, M. "The mentally ill offender: the question of dangerousness." *Prison Journal,* 49(1969), 6-12.

Helpern, M., et al. "Changing patterns of homicide in New York City." *New York State Journal of Medicine,* 72(1972), 2154-2157.

Hentig, H. von "The genetics of murder and seven other crime studies." *Kriminalistik,* 21(1971).

_____"Murder weapons in the homophile sphere." *Archiv fur Kriminologie,* 136(1965), 122-129.

_____"Pre-murderous kindness and post-murder grief." *Journal of Criminal Law, Criminology, and Police Science,* 48(1957), 369-377.

_____"Redhead and outlaw. A study in criminal anthropology." *Journal of Criminal Law, Criminology, and Police Science,* 38(1947), 1-6.

_____"Remarks on the intervention of perpetrator and victim." *Journal of Criminal Law, Criminology, and Police Science,* 31(1940), 303-309.

_____"The suspect. A study in the psychopathology of social standards." *Journal of Criminal Law, Criminology and Police Science,* 39(1948), 19-33.

Hepburn, J. "Subculture violence and the subculture of violence, an old rut or a new road?" *Criminology,* 9(1971), 87-98.

_____and H. Voss. "Patterns of American Homicide: a comparison of Chicago and Philadelphia." *Criminology,* 8(1970), 21-46.

Hewlings, D. "The treatment of murderers." *Howard Journal of Penology and Crime Prevention,* 13(1971), 96-106.

Hienz, H. "YY syndrome forms." *Lancet,* (1964), 155-156.

Hildreth, A. "Body buffer zone and violence. A reassessment and confirmation." *American Journal of Psychiatry,* 127(1971), 1641-1645.

Hill, H., et al. "An MMPI factor analytic study of alcoholics, narcotic addicts and criminals." *Quarterly Journal of Studies on Alcohol,* 23(1962), 411-431.

Hill, J. "Aggression and mental illness," J. Carthy and F. Ebling, *The Natural History of Aggression* (New York, 1964).

_____and D. Pond. "Reflections on one hundred capital cases submitted to electroencephalography." *Journal of Mental Science*, 98(1952), 23-43.

Hinde, R. "Aggression again." *New Society*, 11(1969), 291-292.

_____ "The bases of aggression in animals." *Journal of Psychosomatic Research*, 13(1969), 213-219.

_____ "The nature of aggression." *New Society*, 9(1967), 302-304.

Hivert, P. "The taking of hostages by prison inmates." *Revue Penitentiaire et de Droit Penal et Etudes Criminologiques*, 96(1972), 485-487.

Hoffer, A. "The effect of LSD on chromosomes." *Canadian Medical Association Journal*, 98(1968), 466.

Hollis, W. "On the etiology of criminal homicides—the alcohol factor." *Journal of Police Science and Administration*, 2(1974), 50-53.

Hook, E. "Height and anti-social behavior in XX and XYY boys." *Science*, 172(1971), 284-286.

_____ "Prevalence of XYY and XXY karyotypes in 337 non-retarded young offenders." *New England Journal of Medicine*, 283(1970), 410-411.

Hoover, J. "Violence in American society. A problem in critical concern." *George Washington Law Review*, 36(1967), 407-423.

Hope, K., et al. "Psychological characteristics associated with XYY sex-chromosome complenent in a state mental hospital." *British Journal of Psychiatry*, 113(1967), 495-498.

Hopwood, J. "Child murder and insanity." *Journal of Mental Science*, 73(1927), 95-108.

Hott, L. "Individual and mass aggression: Neo-Freudian point of view." *Beh. Neur.*, 2(1970), 15-16.

Housley, R. "The XYY chromosome complement and criminal conduct." *Delaware State Medical Journal*, 22(1969), 287-301.

Hovland, C., and R. Sears. "Minor studies of aggression: VI correlations of lynchings with economic indices." *Journal of Psychology*, 9(1940), 301-310.

Howell, R. "Differences among behavioral variables, personal characteristics and personality scores of tattooed and non-tattooed prison inmates." *Journal of Research in Crime and Delinquency*, 8(1971), 32-37.

Hoyles, J. "Crimes of violence." *Prison Service Journal*, 9(1969), 37-39.

Hugdens, R. "Murder by a manic depressive." *International Journal of Neuropsychiatry*, 1(1965), 381-383.

Huffman, A. "Violent behavior—possibilities for prediction and control." *Police*, 8(1965), 13-16.

Hughes, J., et al. "A controlled study on the behavior disorders associated with the positive spike phenomenon." *Electroenceph. Clin. Neurophysiol.*, 18(1965), 349-353.

Hunter, H. "Chromatin-positive and XYY boys in approved schools." *Lancet* (1968), 816.

_____ "Klinefelter's syndrome and delinquency." *British Journal of Criminology*, 18(1968), 203-207.

Jableasky, A., et al. "Neuropsychiatric illness and neuropathological findings in a case of Klinefelter's syndrome." *Psychological Medicine*, 1(1970), 18-29.

Jaywardene, C. "Are murderers dangerous?" *Probation and Child Care Journal*,

2(1962), 33-35.

———— "Criminal homicide in Ceylon." *Probation and Child Care,* 3(1964), 15-30.

———— "The death penalty and the safety of Canadian policemen." *Canadian Journal of Criminology and Corrections,* 15(1973), 356-366.

———— "Life or death—society's reaction to murder." *Canadian Journal of Criminology and Corrections,* 15(1973), 265-273.

Johnson, E. "Sociology of confinement-assimilation and the prison rat." *Journal of Criminal Law, Criminology, and Police Science,* 51(1971), 39-44.

Judd, L., et al. "Comparison of the chromosomal patterns obtained from groups of continued users, former users, and non-users of LSD-25." *American Journal of Psychiatry,* 126(1969), 625-635.

Jutrona, F. "Homicides and suicides committed by the insane: medicolegal observations." *Medicine and Society,* 19(1969), 196-204.

Kaada, B. "Brain mechanisms related to aggressive behavior," C. Clemente and D. Lindsley, eds., *Aggression and Defense, Neural Mechanisms and Social Patterns* (Los Angeles, 1967).

Kahn, M. "A comparison of personality, intelligence, and social history of two criminal groups." *Journal of Social Psychology,* 49(1959), 33-40.

———— "A factor-analytic study of personality, intelligence, and history characteristics of murderers." *American Psychologist,* 20(1965), 492.

———— "Psychological test study of a mass murderer." *Journal of Projective Techniques,* 24(1960), 148-160.

———— "Superior performance: IQ murderers as function of overt act or diagnosis." *Journal of Social Psychology,* 76(1968), 113-116.

Kahn, R. "The justification of violence: social problems and social solutions." *Journal of Social Issues,* 28(1972), 115-175.

Kaplan, H. "Toward a general theory of psychosocial deviance. The case of aggressive behavior." *Social Science and Medicine,* 6(1972), 593-617.

Kaplan, S. "Psychophysiology of criminals." *American Psychologist,* 21(1966), 604.

Karpman, B. "Conscience in the psychopath." *American Journal of Orthopsychology,* 18(1948), 455.

———— "Paranoiac murder." *Archives of Criminal Psychodynamics,* 1(1955), 909-939.

———— "A psychoanalytic study of a case of murder." *Psychoanalytic Review,* 38(1951), 139-157.

Keith, C. "The use of the prison code as a defense." *Bulletin of the Menninger Clinic,* 28(1964), 251-258.

Kempe, C., et al. "The battered child syndrome." *Journal of the American Medical Association,* 181(1962), 17-24.

Kendall, R. "Relationship between aggression and depression." *Archives of General Psychiatry,* 22(1970), 308-318.

Kessler, S., and R. Moos. "The XYY karyotype and criminality: a review." *Journal of Psychiatric Research,* 7(1970), 153-170.

Kihlberg, J. "Head injury in automobile accidents," W. Caveness and A. Walker, eds., *Head Injury: Conference Proceedings* (Philadelphia, 1966).

Kilpatrick, J. "Murder in the deep South." *Survey Graphic,* 32(1943), 395-397.

King, F. "Are criminals born or made?" *Australian Police Journal,* 25(1971), 53-55.

Kinzel, A. "Body buffer zone in violent prisoners." *American Journal of Psychology,* 127(1957), 273-279.

Kirkwood, J. "Diagnosing sociopathic personality. Disturbance in the juvenile offender." *Nervous Child,* 11(1955), 28-29.

Kislak, J., and F. Beach. "Inhibition of aggressiveness by ovarian hormones." *Endocrinology,* 56(1955), 684-692.

Kittrie, N. "Will the XYY syndrome abolish guilt?" *Federal Probation,* 35(1971), 26-31.

Klepfisz, A., and J. Racey, "Homicide and LSD." *Journal of the American Medical Association,* 223(1973), 429-430.

Kletschka, H. "Violent behavior associated with brain tumor." *Minnesota Medicine,* 49(1966), 1853-1855.

Knowlton, C. "Violence in New Mexico: a sociological perspective." *California Law Review,* 59(1970), 1054-1084.

Knudsen, K. "Homicide after treatment with lysergic acid." *Acta Psychiatrica Scandinavica,* 40(1964), 389-395.

Koff, G., and T. Langfitt. "Tremoring-induced rage and the limbic system." *Archives Internationales de Pharmacodyname et de Therapie,* 164(1966), 272-283.

Kopernik, L. "The family as the breeding ground of violence." *Correctional Psychiatry and Journal of Social Therapy,* 10(1964), 315-322.

Kozol, H., et al. "The diagnosis and treatment of dangerousness." *Crime and Delinquency,* 18(1972), 371-392.

Kramer, H., et al. "Amphetamine abuse." *Journal of the American Medical Association,* 201(1967), 305-309.

Kraus, J. "Trends in the rates of murder, manslaughter, and rape among male juveniles (N.S. 1956-1959)." *Australian and New Zealand Journal of Criminology,* 5(1972), 146-156.

Kreuz, L. "Assessment of aggressive behavior and plasma testosterone in a young criminal population." *Psychol. Med.,* 34(1972), 321-332.

Kroll, J. "Problem prisoners in the stockade." *Military Police Journal,* 17(1967), 8-10.

Kurland, A. "A comparative study of wife murderers admitted to a state psychiatric hospital." *Journal of Social Therapy,* 1(1955), 7-14.

Lagerspetz, K. "Aggression and aggressiveness in laboratory mice," S. Garattini and E. Sigg, eds., *Aggressive Behavior* (New York, 1969).

———— "Genetic and social causes of aggressive behavior in mice." *Scandinavian Journal of Psychology,* 2(1961), 167-173.

Lalli, M., and S. Turner. "Suicide and homicide: a comparative analysis by race and occupational levels." *Journal of Criminal Law, Criminology, and Police Science,* 59(1968), 191-200.

Lamberti, J. "The sudden murderer. A preliminary report." *Journal of Social Therapy,* 4(1958), 2-15.

Landau, H. "A mental patient with a criminal record: individual liberty vs. public safety." *International Journal of Offender Therapy,* 15(1971), 189-194.

Langner, H. "The making of a murderer." *American Journal of Psychiatry,* 127 (1971), 950-953.

Lanzkron, J. "Murder and insanity." *American Journal of Psychiatry,* 119(1963), 754-758.

———— "Murder as a reaction: paranoid delusions in involutional psychosis and its prevention." *American Journal of Psychiatry*, 118(1961), 426-427.

———— "Psychopathology of the homicidal patient." *Corrective Psychiatry and Journal of Social Therapy*, 10(1964), 142-155.

Laties, V. "Modification of affect, social behavior and performance by sleep deprivation and drugs." *Journal of Psychiatric Research*, 1(1961), 12-25.

Latimer, H. "Murder: a lawyer's look." *Canadian Bar Association Journal*, 3(1972), 4-7

Leakey, L. "Development of aggression in early human and pre-human evolution," C. Clemente and D. Lindsley, eds., *Aggression and Defense* (Berkeley, Calif., 1967).

Leeke, W. "Collective violence in correctional institutions." *American Journal of Corrections*, 33(1971), 12-16.

Leff, J. "XYY and intelligence." *Lancet* (1968), 645.

Lefkowitz, N. "Physique and obstreperous behavior." *Journal of Clinical Psychology*, 347(1966), 51-57.

Le Maire, L. "Danish experience regarding the castration of sexual offenders." *Journal of Criminal Law and Criminology*, 47(1956), 294-310.

Lennox, W. "The genetics of epilepsy." *American Journal of Psychiatry*, 103(1947), 457-462.

Le Roux, L., and L. Smith. "Violent deaths and alcoholic intoxication." *Journal of Forensic Medicine*, 11(1964), 131-147.

Lester, D. "Suicide and homicide. Bias in the examination of the relationship between suicide and homicide rates." *Soc. Psych.*, 6(1971), 80-82.

———— "Suicide, homicide and color shading response on the Rorschach." *Perc. Mot. Skills*, 35(1972), 56-62.

Lette, M. "Prison ecology: observations on hierarchical structure in a closed environment." *Annales Internationales de Criminologie*, 10(1971), 277-283.

Levin, Y., and A. Lindesmith. "English ecology and criminology of the past century." *Journal of Criminal Law, Criminology and Police Science*, 27(1937), 801-816.

Leyhausen, P. "The sane community—a density problem?" *Discovery* (1965), 27-33.

Liber, B. "Psychopathic personalities. Failures and criminals." *New York State Journal of Medicine*, 53(1953), 1088-1094.

Lidberg, L. "Frequency of concussion and type of criminality: a preliminary report." *Acta Psychiatrica Scandinavica*, 47(1971).

Liddell, D. "Observation on epileptic automatism in a mental hospital population." *Journal of Mental Science*, 99(1953), 731-748.

Lieber, A. "Homicides and the lunar cycle: toward a theory of lunar influence on human emotional disturbance." *American Journal of Psychiatry*, 129(1972), 69-74.

Lincoln, A. "Observers' evaluations of the victim and the attacker in an aggressive incident." *Journal of Personality and Social Psychology*, 22(1972), 202-210.

Lion, J., et al. "The self-referred violent patient." *Journal of the American Medical Association*, 205(1968), 503-505.

———— et al. "Violent patients in the emergency room." *American Journal of Psychiatry*, 125(1968-1969), 1706-1711.

Lipton, H. "Situational murder due to emotional stress." *Acta Criminologica et Medicinae Legalis Japonica*, 29(1963), 1-2.

Little, J. "Who is the deadly drinking driver?" *Journal of Criminal Law, Criminology and Police Science*, 59(1968), 619-623.

Livingston, S. "Epilepsy and murder." *Journal of the American Medical Association,* 188(1964), 172.

Logan, C. "General deterrent effects of imprisonment." *Social Forces,* 51(1972), 64-73.

Lorenz, K. "Ritualized fighting," J. Carthy and F. Ebbing, eds., *The Natural History of Aggression* (London, 1964).

Lottier, S. "Distribution of criminal offenses in metropolitan regions." *Journal of Criminal Law and Criminology,* 29(1938), 37-50.

"LSD and chromosomes." *British Medical Journal,* 2(1968), 778-779.

Lubs, H., and F. Ruddle. "Chromosomal abnormalities in the human population: estimates of rates in New Haven newborn study." *Science,* 169(1970), 495-497.

Luke, J. "Strangulation as a method of homicide." *Archives of Pathology,* 83(1967), 64-70.

Lyle, W. "The Cornell index as a screening device with institutionalized offenders." *British Journal of Criminology,* 8(1966), 295-300.

McDanal, C. "A survey among tall male prisoners for the XYY karyotype." *Tex. Rep. Biol. Med.,* 28(1970), 397-398.

McDermaid, G. "Psychopathology of infanticide." *Journal of Clinical and Experimental Psychopathology,* 16(1955), 22-41.

_____ and E. Winkler. "Psychiatric study of homicide cases." *Journal of Clinical Psychopathology,* 11(1950), 93-146.

MacDonald, J. "Homicidal threats." *American Journal of Psychiatry,* 124(1967), 161-168.

_____ "Suicide and homicide by automobile." *American Journal of Psychiatry,* 121(1964), 366-370.

_____ "The threat to kill." *American Journal of Psychiatry,* 120(1963), 125-130.

McGeorge, J. "Alcohol and crime." *Medicine, Science and the Law,* 3(1963), 27-48.

McGregor, R. "The psychopath." *Probation,* 18(1972), 25-27.

MacKay, E. "Clinical significance of disorders of the sex chromosomes." *Medical Journal of Australia,* 54(1967), 552-554.

McKnight, C., et al. "Mental illness and homicide." *Canadian Medical Association Journal,* 11(1966), 91-98.

Mallick, S., and B. McCandless. "A study of catharsis of aggression," L. Berkowitz, ed., *Roots of Aggression* (New York, 1969).

Malquist, C. "Premonitory signs of homicidal aggression in juveniles." *American Journal of Psychiatry,* 128(1971), 461-465.

Mandel, J. "Hashish, assassins and the love of God." *Issues in Criminology,* 2(1966), 149-156.

Manne, S. "Differences between performance IQ and verbal IQ in a severely sociopathic population." *Journal of Clinical Psychology,* 18(1962), 73-77.

_____ and D. Rosenthal. "IQ and age of first commitment of dangerous offenders." *Correctional Psychologist,* 4(1971), 220-229.

Marinello, M. "A study of the XYY syndrome in tall men and juvenile delinquents." *Journal of the American Medical Association,* 4(1969), 321-325.

Mark, V. "Brain disease and violent behavior." *Neuroopthamology Symposium,* 4(1968), 282-287.

Marohn, R. "A hospital riot: its determinants and implications for treatment." *American Journal of Psychiatry,* 130(1973), 631-636.

Martinson, R. "Collective behavior in Attica." *Federal Probation,* 36(1972), 3-7.

Masters, F. "The Quasimodo complex." *British Journal of Plastic Surgery*, 20(1967), 204-210.

Matthew, J. "Six and fourteen dysthymia and the ego: a case of near homicide." *Journal of Neurobiology*, 5(1964), 490-494.

Matthews, L. "Overt fighting in mammals," J. Carthy and F. Eblings, eds., *The Natural History of Aggression* (London, 1964).

Mattick, H. "The prosaic sources of prison violence." *Australian and New Zealand Journal of Criminology*, 5(1973), 12-20.

Maughs, S. "The psychopathic personality—review of the literature." *Progress in Neurology and Psychiatry*, Vol. 11 (New York, 1956).

Mead, M. "Cultural factors in the cause and prevention of pathological homicide." *Bulletin of the Menninger Clinic*, 28(1964), 11-22.

Megargee, E. "Assault with intent to kill. New insights into the psychology of the killer." *Transaction*, 2(1965), 504-512.

––––––– "The prediction of violence with psychological tests," C. Spielberger, ed., *Current Topics in Clinical and Community Psychology*, Vol. 1 (New York, 1970).

––––––– and G. Mendelsohn. "A cross-validation of twelve MMPI indices of hostility and control." *Journal of Abnormal and Social Psychology*, 65(1962), 431-438.

Melnyk, J., et al. "XYY survey of an institution for sex offenders and the mentally ill." *Nature*, 224(1969), 369.

Menninger, K., and M. Mayman. "Episodic dyscontrol: a third order of stress adaptation." *Bulletin of the Menninger Clinic*, 20(1956), 153.

Merton, R. "Social structure and anomie," M. Wolfgang et al., eds., *The Sociology of Crime and Delinquency* (New York, 1962).

Messinger, E., and A. Zitrin. "A statistical study of criminal drug addicts: psychosis, psychoneurosis, mental deficiency and personality types." *Crime and Delinquency*, 11(1965), 283-292.

Meunier, P., and H. Schwartz. "Beyond Attica: prison reform in New York State 1971-73." *Cornell Law Review*, 58(1973), 924-1023.

Meyer, A., et al. "Men who kill women." *Journal of Clinical Psychopathology*, 7(1946), 441-472; 8(1947), 481-517.

Meyers, A. "Murder and non-negligent manslaughters: a statistical study." *St. Louis University Law Journal*, 3(1954), 18-34.

Michaels, J. "Enuresis in murderous aggressive children and adolescents." *Archives of General Psychiatry*, 5(1961), 490-493.

Michaux, M. "Psychodiagnostic follow-up of a juvenile sex murderer." *Psych. Rev.*, 50(1963), 93-114.

Mikkelsen, M. "Sex chromosome abnormalities in mentally retarded criminals." *Journal of Legal Medicine*, 69(1971), 157-160.

Miller, J. "Individual and mass aggression." *Beh. Neur.*, 2(1970), 12-13.

Miller, W. "Violent crimes in city gangs." *Annals of the American Academy of Political and Social Science*, 364(1966), 96-112.

Molof, M. "Differences between assaultive and non-assaultive juvenile offenders in the California Youth Authority," State of California Department of the Youth Authority, *Research Report No. 51* (1967).

Money, J. "Impulse aggression and sexuality in the XYY syndrome." *St. Johns Law Review*, 44(1969), 220-235.

––––––– et al. "Impulse aggression and sexuality in the XYY syndrome." *Digest of Neurology and Psychiatry*, 38(1971), 400.

Montagu, A. "Chromosomes and crime." *Psychology Today,* 2(1968), 43-49.

Moos, R. "The assessment of the social climates of correctional institutions." *Journal of Research in Crime and Delinquency,* 5(1968), 174-188.

Moran, R. "Criminal homicide, external restraint and the subculture of violence." *Criminology,* 8(1971), 357-374.

Morris, G. "Irrational beliefs of prison inmates." *Canadian Journal of Criminology and Corrections,* 16(1974), 53-59.

Morris, N. "Psychiatry and the dangerous criminal." *Southern California Law Review,* 41(1968), 514-547.

Morris, P. "Staff problems in a maximum security prison." *Prison Service Journal,* 2(1963), 3-15.

Morrison, W. "Criminal homicide and the death penalty in Canada: time for reassessment and new directions. Toward a typology of homicide." *Canadian Journal of Criminology and Corrections,* 15(1973), 367-379.

Morrow, W. "Prejudice and the offenses of penal-psychiatric patients." *Journal of Clinical Psychology,* 20(1964), 218-225.

———— "A psychodynamic analysis of the crimes of prejudiced and unprejudiced male prisoners." *Bulletin of the Menninger Clinic,* 13(1949), 204-212.

Morton, J. "Female homicides." *Journal of Mental Science,* 80(1934), 64-74.

———— "Parkhurst and after." *New Society,* 16(1970), 223-234.

Moses, E. "Differentials in crime rates between Negroes and whites; based on comparisons of four socio-economically equated areas." *American Sociological Review,* 12(1947), 411-420.

Mosher, D., et al. "The body image of tattooed prisoners." *Journal of Clinical Psychology,* 23(1967), 31-32.

Moychan, J., et al. "Explaining the stunning murder-suicide by a quiet family man." *Journal of the American Medical Association,* 221(1972), 20.

Munch, J. "Marijuana and crime." *Bulletin on Narcotics,* 18(1966), 15-22.

Narabayashi, H., and M. Uns. "Long range results in stereotaxic amygdalotomy for behaviour disorders." *Confina Neurologica,* 27(1966), 168-171.

Neiberg, N. "Murder and suicide." *Archives of Criminal Psychodynamics,* 4(1961), 253-268.

Neustatter, W. "Psychiatric aspects of diminished responsibility in murder." *Medico-Legal Journal,* 28(1960), 92-101.

———— "The state of mind in murder." *Lancet* (1965), 861-863.

Nicol, A. "The relationship of alcoholism to violent behavior resulting in long-term imprisonment." *British Journal of Psychiatry,* 123(1973), 47-51.

———— et al. "The quantitative assessment of violence in adult and young offenders." *Medicine, Science and Law,* 12(1972), 275-282.

Nielsen, J. "Incidence of chromosome aberration among males in a Danish youth prison." *Acta Psychiatrica Scandinavica,* 48(1972), 87-102.

———— "A psychiatric-psychological study of patients with the XYY syndrome found outside of institutions." *Acta Psychiatrica Scandinavica,* 49(1973), 159-168.

———— "The XYY syndrome in a mental hospital: genetically determined criminality." *British Journal of Criminology,* 8(1966), 186-203.

———— "XYY chromosomal constitution in criminal psychopaths." *Lancet* (1968), 576.

Nordlicht, S. "Determinants of violence." *New York State Journal of Medicine,*

72(1972), 2163-2165.

Nye, F. "Child adjustment in broken and unhappy unbroken homes." *Marriage and Family Living*, 19(1957), 356-361.

Oberschall, A. "Group violence. Some hypotheses and empirical uniformities." *Law and Society Review*, 5(1970), 61-92.

O'Connel, B. "Amnesia and homicide—a study of 50 murderers." *British Journal of Delinquency*, 10(1960), 262-276.

Oda, S., and O. Hilcata. "A psychiatric report on a case of sexual homicide." *Acta Criminologica et Medicinae Legalis Japonica*, 36(1970), 107-117.

O'Donnell, J. "Narcotic addiction and crime." *Social Problems*, 13(1966), 374-385.

O'Regan, R. "Duress and murder." *Modern Law Review*, 35(1972), 596-605.

Ostoja, S. "Suicide and homicide committed by the insane: the crime of the insane patient against the doctor." *Medicine and Society*, 19(1969), 210-211.

Owen, D. "The 47 XYY male. A review." *Psychiatric Bulletin*, 78(1972), 209-233.

Palmer, S. "Murder and suicide in forty non-literate societies." *Journal of Criminal Law, Criminology, and Police Science*, 56(1965), 320-324.

———. "Psychological frustrations. A comparison of murderers and their brothers." M. Wolfgang, ed., *Studies in Homicide* (New York, 1967).

Peizer, S. "What do prisons do anyway?" *Police*, 6(1961), 6-10.

Perdue, W. "A preliminary investigation into uxoricide." *Diseases of the Nervous System*, 27(1966), 808-811.

———. "Rorschach responses of 100 murderers." *Correctional Psychiatry and Journal of Social Therapy*, 10(1964), 323-328.

———. "A study of the Rorschach records of forty-seven murderers." *Publication J. Soc. Ther.*, 7(1961), 158-167.

———. and D. Lester. "Temperamentally suited to kill: the personality of murderers." *Corrective and Social Psychiatry and Journal of Applied Behavior Therapy*, 20(1974), 13-15.

"Personality of murderesses." *Journal of the American Medical Association*, 25 (1968), 106.

Peterson, B., and C. Petty. "Sudden natural death among automobile drivers." *Journal of Forensic Sciences*, 7(1962), 274-285.

Pierce, D. "A cross-validation of the MMPI habitual criminalism scale." *Correctional Psychologist*, 4(1971), 183-187.

———. "The escapism scale of the MMPI as a predictive index." *Correctional Psychologist*, 4(1971), 230-232.

Pittman, D., and W. Handy. "Patterns in criminal aggravated assault," M. Clinard and R. Quinney, eds., *Criminal Behavior Systems: A Typology* (New York, 1967).

"Plea in XYY case fails." *NCCD News*, 48(1969), 4.

Podolsky, E. "The alcoholic murderer." *Pakistan Medical Journal*, 12(1961).

———. "The chemistry of murder." *Pakistan Medical Journal*, 15(1964), 9-14.

———. "The diseased brain and homicide." *Correctional Psychiatry and Journal of Social Therapy*, 11(1965), 91-94.

———. "The electrophysiology of homicide." *Diseases of the Nervous System*, 23(1962), 146-148.

———. "Jealousy as a motive in homicide." *Diseases of the Nervous System*, 22(1961), 438-441.

———. "The manic murderer." *Corrective Psychiatry and Journal of Social Thera-*

py, 10(1964), 213-217.

_____ "Mind of the murderer." *Journal of Criminal Law, Criminology, and Police Science,* 45(1954), 48-50.

_____ "Notes on motiveless murder." *International Journal of Social Psychiatry,* 1(1956), 42-45.

_____ "The psychodynamics of criminal behavior." *International Journal of Neuropsychiatry,* 2(1966), 166-174.

_____ "Sexual violence." *Medical Digest,* 34(1966), 60-63.

_____ "The sociopathic alcoholic." *Quarterly Journal of Studies on Alcohol,* 21(1960), 292-297.

_____ "Somnambulistic homicide." *Medicine, Science, and the Law,* 1(1961), 260-265.

_____ "Somnambulistic homicide." *American Journal of Psychiatry,* 121(1964), 191-192.

Pokorny, A. "A comparison of homicides in two cities." *Journal of Criminal Law, Criminology, and Police Science,* 56(1965), 479-487.

_____ "Geomagnetic fluctuations and disturbed behavior." *Journal of Nervous and Mental Diseases,* 143(1966), 140-151.

_____ "Human violence: a comparison of homicide, aggravated assault, suicide and attempted suicide." *Journal of Criminal Law, Criminology, and Police Science,* 56(1965), 488-497.

_____ "Homicide and weather." *American Journal of Psychiatry,* 120(1964), 806-808.

Porterfield, A. "Indices of suicide and homicide by states and cities." *American Sociological Review,* 14(1949), 481-490.

_____ "Traffic fatalities, suicide and homicide." *American Sociological Review,* 25(1960), 897-901.

Post, R. "The relationship of tattoos to personality disorders." *Journal of Criminal Law, Criminology and Police Science,* 59(1968), 516-524.

Power, D. "Subnormality and crime: II." *Medicine, Science and the Law,* 9(1969), 162-171.

Price, D. "Necrophilia complicating a case of homicide." *Medicine, Science and the Law,* 3(1963), 121-131.

Price, W. "Criminal patients with XXY sex chromosome complement." *Lancet* (1966), 565-566.

_____ "Sex chromosome abnormalities: How strong is the link with crime?" *Manitoba Medical Review,* 48(1968), 26-27.

Quinney, R. "Suicide, homicide, and economic development." *Social Forces,* 43 (1965), 401-406.

Rabin, A. "Homicide and attempted suicide. A Rorschach study." *American Journal of Orthopsychiatry,* 16(1946), 516-524.

_____ and J. Hess. "Attitudes of prison personnel and inmates to crime and punishment." *Journal of Offender Therapy,* 10(1960), 551-553.

Raizen, K. "A case of matricide-patricide." *British Journal of Delinquency,* 10 (1960), 277-294.

Randolph, M. "A comparison of social and solitary male delinquents." *Journal of Cons. Psych.,* 25(1961), 293-295.

Rapp, J. "Sudden death in the gay world." *Medicine, Science, and the Law*, 10(1970) 189-191.

Rappeport, J., and G. Lassen. "Dangerousness arrest rate comparisons of discharged psychiatric patients." *American Journal of Psychiatry*, 121(1965), 776-783.

_____ "The dangerousness of female patients. A comparison of the arrest rate of discharged psychiatric patients and the general population." *American Journal of Psychiatry*, 123(1967), 413-419.

_____ et al. "A review of the literature on the dangerousness of the mentally ill," J. Rappeport, ed., *Clinical Evaluation of the Dangerousness of the Mentally Ill* (Springfield, Ill. 1967).

Raven, A. "A theory of murder." *American Sociological Review*, 22(1930), 108-118.

Raynes, A., et al. "Effect of alcohol and congeners on aggressive responsive in *Betta splendens.*" *Quarterly Journal of Studies on Alcohol*, 5(1970), 130-135.

Reich, P., and R. Hepps. "Homicide during a psychosis induced by LSD." *Journal of the American Medical Association*, 219(1972), 869-871.

Reichard, S. "Murder and suicide as defense against schizophrenic psychosis." *Journal of Clinical Psychology*, 11(1950), 149-163.

Reinhardt, J. "The crypto-sex murderer." *Criminologist*, 3(1968), 67-71.

_____ "The dismal tunnel: depression before murder." *International Journal of Offender Therapy*, 17(1973), 246-249.

_____ "The wish to confess." *Police*, 14(1969), 50-52.

Reiss, A. "The social integration of queers and peers." *Social Problems*, 9(1961), 102-120.

Reitalu, J. "Chromosome studies in connection with sex chromosomal deviations in man." *Hereditas*, 59(1968), 1-48.

Resnick, P. "Child murder by parents: a psychiatric review of filicide.' *American Journal of Psychiatry*, 126(1969), 325-334.

_____ "Murder of the newborn. A psychiatric review of neonaticide." *American Journal of Psychiatry*, 126(1970), 1414-1420.

Rettig, S. "Ethical risk sensitivity of male prisoners." *British Journal of Criminology*, 4(1964), 582-590.

Revitch, E. "Sex murder and the potential sex murderer." *Diseases of the Nervous System*, 26(1965), 640-648.

Richard, S., and C. Tillman. "Murder and suicide as a defense against schizophrenic psychoses." *Journal of Clinical Psychopathology*, 11(1950), 149.

Richardson, F. "The domestic murderer. The regime of Kingston (Portsmouth)." *Prison Service Journal*, 8(1972), 9-11.

Richmond, R. "The homosexual in prison." *Canadian Journal of Corrections* 12 (1970), 553-555.

Robbins, P. "Community violence and aggression in dreams. An observation." *Perc. Mot. Skills*, 29(1969), 41-42.

Roberts, B. "On the origins and resolution of English working-class protest " H. Graham and T. Gurr, eds., *The History of Violence in America* (New York. 1969).

Robin, D. "Justifiable homicide by police officers." *Journal of Criminal Law, Criminology, and Police Science*, 54(1963), 225-231.

Robins, L. "Negro homicide victims—who will they be?" *Transaction*, 5(1968), 15-19.

Roebuck, J. "Chromosomes and the criminal." *Journal of Social Therapy*, 15(1969), 103-117.

———— "The jack-of-all-trades." *Crime and Delinquency*, 8(1962), 172-181.

———— and R. Johnson. "The Negro drinker and assaulter as a criminal type." *Crime and Delinquency*, 8(1962), 21-33.

Rose, G. "Screen memories in homicidal acting out." *Psychiatric Quarterly*, 29 (1960), 328-343.

Rosenberg, P. "Management of disturbed adolescents." *Diseases of the Nervous System*, 27(1966), 60-61.

Rosenow, E. "Influence of streptococcal infections on the compulsive behavior of criminals." *Postgraduate Medicine*, 10(1951), 422-434.

Rosenthal, A. "Violence is predictable." *Today's Health*, 48(1970), 56-57.

Ross, H. "Traffic law violation: a folk crime." *Social Problems*, 8(1961), 231-241.

Roth, M. "Human violence as viewed from the psychiatric clinic." *American Journal of Psychiatry*, 128(1972), 1043-1056.

Rothballer, A. "Aggression, defense and neurohumors," C. Clemente and D. Lindsley, eds., *Aggression and Defense* (Berkeley, Calif. 1967).

Rothenberg, A. "On anger." *American Journal of Psychiatry*, 128(1972), 454-460.

Rothenberg, M. "Violence and children." *Mental Hygiene*, 53(1969), 539-544.

Rubin, B. "Prediction of dangerousness in mentally ill criminals." *Archives of General Psychiatry*, 27(1972), 397-407.

Russell, D. "Juvenile murderers." *International Journal of Offender Therapy and Comp. Crim.*, 17(1973), 235-239.

———— "A study of juvenile murderers." *Journal of Offender Therapy*, 9(1965), 55-68.

Sabath, G. "Characteristics of contemporary violence." *Correctional Psychiatry and Journal of Social Therapy*, 12(1966), 371-379.

Sadoff, R. "Clinical observations on parricide." *Psychiatric Quarterly*, 40(1971), 305-315.

Sagarin, E. "Voluntary associations among social deviants." *Criminologica*, 5(1967), 3-22.

Salzman, L. "Psychodynamics of a case of murder." *Comprehensive Psychiatry*, 3(1962), 152-169.

Sandberg, A., et al. "An XYY human male." *Lancet* (1961), 488-489.

Sanders, J. "Euthanasia. None dare call it murder." *Journal of Criminal Law, Criminology, and Police Science*, 60(1969), 351-359.

Sandler, H. "Therapy with violent psychopaths in an Indian prison community." *International Journal of Offender Therapy*, 14(1970), 138-144.

Sannito, T. "Relationship between the WAIS and indices of sociopathy in an incarcerated female population." *Journal of Research in Crime and Delinquency*, 3(1966), 63-70.

Sano, K., et al. "Posterior-medial hypothalamotomy in the treatment of aggressive behaviors." *Confina Neurologica*, 27(1966), 164-167.

Sarbin, T. "The dangerous individual: an outcome of social identity transformation." *British Journal of Criminology*, 7(1967), 285-295.

———— "Demonism revisited: the XYY chromosomal anomaly." *Issues in Criminology*, 5(1970), 195-207.

———— "An effort to identify assault-prone offenders." *Journal of Research in Crime and Delinquency*, 5(1968), 66-71.

_____ "Resolution of binocular rivalry as a means of identifying violence prone offenders." *Journal of Criminal Law, Criminology, and Police Science,* 60(1969), 345-350.

Sargent, D. "Children who kill. A family conspiracy." *Social Work,* 7(1962), 35-42.

Satten, J., et al. "Murder without apparent motive." *American Journal of Psychiatry,* 117(1960), 48-53.

Saul, L. "Personal and social psychopathology and the primary prevention of violence." *American Journal of Psychiatry,* 128(1972), 1578-1581.

Schilder, P. "The attitude of murderers toward death." *Abnormal and Social Psychology,* 31(1936), 348.

Schmid, C. "A study of homicides in Seattle, 1914-1924." *Social Forces,* 4(1926), 745-756.

Schneider, H. "Euthanasia. A comparative examination of its place within the scope of the criminal law." *Criminologica,* 7(1969), 25-38.

Schuessler, K. "Personality characteristics of criminals." *American Journal of Sociology,* 55(1950), 476-484.

Schulman, I. "Dynamics and treatment of anti-social psychopathology in adolescents." *Nervous Child,* 11(1955), 35-41.

Schwab, R., et al. "Treatment of intractable temporal lobe epilepsy by stereotactic amygdala lesions." *Transactions of the American Neurological Association* (1965), 12-19.

Schwade, E., and S. Geiger. "Abnormal EEG findings in severe behavior disorder." *Diseases of the Nervous System,* 17(1956), 307-317.

_____ and S. Geiger. "Severe behavior disorders with abnormal electroencephalograms." *Diseases of the Nervous System,* 21(1960), 616-620.

_____ and O. Otto. "Homicide as a manifestation of thalamic or hypothalamic disorder with abnormal EEG findings." *Wisconsin Medical Journal,* 52(1953), 171-174.

Schwartz, B. "Deprivation of privacy as a functional prerequisite. The case of prison." *Journal of Criminal Law, Criminology and Police Science,* 63(1972), 229-239.

Scott, J. "Biology and human aggression." *American Journal of Orthopsychiatry,* 40(1969), 568-576.

_____ "Dominance and the frustration-aggression hypothesis." *Physiological Zoology,* 21(1948), 31-39.

_____ "Hostility and aggression in animals," E. Bliss, ed., *Roots of Behavior* (New York, 1962).

_____ and J. Hisson. "Changing the delinquent subculture: a sociological approach." *Crime and Delinquency,* 14(1969), 599-610.

Scott, P. "Fatal battered baby cases." *Medicine, Science and the Law,* 13(1973), 197-206.

_____ "Offenders, drunkenness and murder." *British Journal of Addictions,* 63(1968), 221-226.

_____ "Parents who kill their children." *Medicine, Science and the Law,* 13 (1973), 120-126.

_____ and J. Kahn. "An XYY patient of above average intelligence as a basis for the review of the psychopathology medico-legal implications of the syndrome and possibilities for prevention," D. West, ed., *Psychopathic Offenders* (Cambridge, England, 1968).

Sears, R. "Relation of early socialization experiences to aggression." *Journal of*

Abnormal and Social Psychology, 63(1961), 461-465.

———et al. "Minor studies of aggression. I. Measurement of aggressive behaviour." *Journal of Psychology,* 9(1940), 275-295.

Seizer, M. "Personality versus intoxication as a critical factor in accidents caused by alcoholic drivers." *Journals of Nervous and Mental Diseases,* 132(1966), 298-303.

Seitz, S. "Firearms, homicides and gun control effectiveness." *Law and Society Review,* 6(1972), 595-613.

Selling, L. "The psychopathology of the 'hit and run' driver." *American Journal of Psychiatry,* 98(1941), 93-98.

Serafetinides, E. "Aggressiveness in temporal lobe epileptics and its relation to cerebral dysfunction and environmental factors." *Epilepsia,* 6(1965), 33-42.

Seward, J. "Aggressive behavior in the rat. I. General characteristics: age and sex differences." *Journal of Comparative Psychology,* 38(1945), 175-197.

"Sex chromosomes and crime." *Ann. Int. Med.,* 69(1968), 399-401.

Shah, S. "Recent developments in human genetics and their implications for problems of social deviance." *National Foundation for Birth Defects,* 8(1972), 21-33.

Shenken, L. "The implications of ego psychology for a motive-less murder." *J. Amer. Acad. Child Psychiat.,* 3(1964), 741-751.

Shapland, P. "Thoughts on disturbances in prison." *Prison Service Journal,* 11(1973), 18-20.

Sheppard, C. "The violent offender: let's examine the taboo." *Federal Probations,* 35(1971), 12-19.

Shepherd, M. "Morbid jealousy: some clinical and social aspects of a psychiatric symptom." *Journal of Mental Science,* 107(1961), 687-704.

Shinochara, M. "MMPI study of three types of delinquents." *Journal of Clinical Psychology,* 23(1967), 156-163.

Shoham, S. "Point of no return: some situational aspects of violence." *Prison Journal,* 48(1968), 29-33.

Shore, M. "Psychological theories of the causes of antisocial behavior." *Crime and Delinquency,* 17(1971), 456-468.

Short, J. "On collective violence; introduction and overview." *Annals of the American Academy of Political and Social Science,* 39(1970), 1-8.

Shotwell, A. "A study of psychopathic delinquency." *American Journal of Ment. Def.,* 51(1946), 57-62.

Shupe, L. "Alcohol and crime: a study of the urine alcohol concentration found in 882 persons arrested during or immediately after the commission of a felony." *Journal of Criminal Law, Criminology and Police Science,* 44(1954), 661-664.

Silverman, D. "The psychotic criminal: a study of 500 cases." *Journal of Clinical Psychiatry,* 8(1946), 301-327.

Simmons, J. "On maintaining deviant belief systems. A case study." *Social Problems,* 11(1964), 250-256.

Sinclair, I., and B. Chapman. "A typological and dimensional study of a sample of prisoners." *British Journal of Criminology,* 13(1973), 341-353.

Sirico, J. "Prisoner classification and administrative decision making." *Texas Law Review,* 50(1972), 1229-1254.

Skelton, W. "Prison riot. Assaulters vs. defenders." *Archives of General Psychology,* 21(1969), 359-362.

Skrzypek, G. "Effect of perceptual isolation and arousal on anxiety complexity preference and novelty preference in psychopathic and neurotic delinquency." *Journal of Abnormal Psychiatry,* 8(1971), 375-395.

Slawski, C. "Crime causation. Toward a field synthesis." *Criminology,* 8(1971), 375-395.

Small, J. "The organic dimension of crime." *Archives of General Psychology,* 15 (1966), 82-89.

Smith, S. "The adolescent murderer. A psychodynamic interpretation." *Archives of General Psychology,* 13(1965), 310-319.

Smykal, A. "Etiological studies of psychopathic personality." *Journal of Criminal Law, Criminology and Police Science,* 7(1951), 299-316.

Solfen, P. "Violence in prison." *Delinquency and Society,* 2(1967), 51-53.

Solomon, P. "The burden of responsibility in suicide and homicide." *Journal of the American Medical Association,* 199(1967), 321-324.

_____ "Medical aspects of violence." *Cal. Med.,* 114(1971), 19-24.

Spain, D., et al. "Alcohol and violent death. A one year study of consecutive cases in a representative community." *Journal of the American Medical Association,* 146(1951), 334-335.

Spitzer, S. "Cognitive organization of sociopaths and normal criminal offenders." *Journal of Research in Crime and Delinquency,* 31(1966), 57-62.

Stachnik, T., et al. "Reinforcement of aggression through intracranial stimulation." *Psychonomic Science,* 6(1965), 101-102.

Stainbrook, E. "Trauma and human violence." *J. Trauma,* 10(1970), 25-31.

Stamp, E., and W. Gilbert. "Experimental MMPI scales and other predictions of institutional adjustments." *Correctional Psychologist,* 5(1972), 141-154.

Stanton, J. "Murderers on parole." *Crime and Delinquency,* 15(1969), 149-155.

_____ "Personality make-up of offenders." *American Journal of Corrections,* 22(1960), 19-22.

Stearns, A. "Homicide in Massachusetts." *American Journal of Psychiatry,* 4(1925), 725-749.

_____ "Murder by adolescents with obscure motivation." *American Journal of Psychiatry,* 114(1957), 303-305.

Stefanowicz, J. "Ethical risk-taking and sociopathy in incarcerated females." *Correctional Psychologist,* 9(1971), 138-152.

Stenchever, M. "A normal XYY man." *Lancet* (1969), 680.

Stengel, E. "Suicide in prison: the gesture and the risk." *Prison Service Journal,* 2(1971), 13-14.

Straus, J. and M. "Suicide, homicide and social structure in Ceylon." *American Journal of Sociology,* 58(1953), 461-469.

Studt, E. "The nature of hard-to-reach groups." *Children,* 4(1957), 219-224.

Sturup, G. "The psychology of murderers." *Irish Medical Association Journal,* 54 (1964), 27-32.

_____ "Will this man be dangerous?" *International Psychiatry Clinics,* 5(1968), 5-18.

Stutte, H. "Criminal deviations under the influence of sexual hormones." *Monatsschrift fur Kriminologie und Strafrechtsreform,* 50(1967), 153-162.

Sutherland, G., and A. Bartholomew. "Chromosome survey in a mental deficiency security ward." *Australian and New Zealand Journal of Criminology,* 4(1971), 82-85.

Sutker, P., et al. "Porteus maze test qualitative performance in pure sociopaths, prison normals and antisocial psychotics." *Journal of Clinical Psychology,* 28 (1972), 349-353.

Svalastoga, K. "Homicide and social contact in Denmark." *American Journal of Sociology,* 62(1956), 37-41.

Sweet, W., et al. "The relationship of violent behaviour to focal cerebral disease," S. Garattini and E. Sigg, eds., *Aggressive Behaviour* (New York, 1969).

Taft, P., and P. Ross. "American labor violence: its causes, character and outcome," H. Graham and T. Gurr, eds., *The History of Violence in America* (New York, 1969).

Tanay, E. "Forensic psychiatry in the legal defense of murder." *Journal of Forensic Science,* 16(1972), 15-24.

———— "Psychiatric aspects of homicide prevention." *American Journal of Psychiatry,* 128(1972), 815-818.

———— "Psychiatric study of homicide." *American Journal of Psychiatry,* 125 (1969), 1252-1258.

Taylor, A. "A brief criminal attitude scale." *Journal of Criminal Law, Criminology and Police Science,* 59(1968), 34-40.

Taylor, R. "The individual and aggression in institutions." *Prison Service Journal,* 11(1973), 16-18.

Tech, J. "The changing psychopathology of amok." *Psychiatry,* 35(1972), 345-351.

Telfer, M. "Incidence of gross chromosomal errors among tall criminal American males." *Science,* 178(1968), 1249-1250.

———— "Diagnosis of gross chromosomal errors in institutional population." *Pennsylvania Psychiatric Quarterly,* 7(1967), 3-13.

———— "YY syndrome in an American Negro." *Lancet* (1968), 95.

Thomas, H. "The dangerous offender." *Syracuse Law Review,* 14(1963), 576-585.

Thomas, J. "Killed on duty: an analysis of murders of English prison service staff since 1850." *Prison Service Journal,* 7(1972), 9-10.

Thouless, R. "Aggression in nature and society." *British Journal of Medical Psychology,* 22(1949), 161-165.

Thurrell, R. "Psychosis in prison." *Journal of Criminal Law, Criminology and Police Science,* 56(1965), 271.

Tillman, W., and G. Hobbs. "The accident-prone automobile driver." *American Journal of Psychiatry,* 106(1949), 321-331.

Tinbergen, N. "On war and peace in animals and man." *Science,* 160(1968), 1411-1418.

Tinklenberg, J., and R. Stillman. "Drug use and violence," D. Daniels et al., eds., *Violence and the Struggle for Existence* (Boston, 1970).

Tittle, C. "Inmate organization: sex differentiation and the influence of criminal subcultures." *American Sociological Review,* 34(1969), 492-505.

———— and D. Tittle. "Social organization of prisoners: an empirical test." *Social Forces,* 43(1964), 216-221.

Toby, J. "Criminal motivation. A sociological analysis." *British Journal of Criminology,* 2(1962), 317-336.

Toch, H. "The care and feeding of typologies and labels." *Federal Probation,* 34 (1970), 15-19.

———— "The social psychology of violence," E. Megargee and J. Hokanson, eds., *The Dynamics of Aggression* (New York, 1970).

Train, G. "Homicidal psychosis while under ACTH corticosteroid therapy for pemphigus vulgaris during involution." *Psychosomatics*, 3(1962), 317-322.

Treffert, D. "The psychiatric patient with an EEG temporal lobe focus." *American Journal of Psychiatry*, 120(1964), 765-771.

Tutman, J. "The murderess." *Police*, 15(1971), 16-22.

Uehling, H. "Crime breeds on smothered feelings." *Federal Probation*, 30(1966), 11-17.

Usher, A. "The case of the disembowelled doll—a multiple murder." *Medicine, Science and the Law*, 7(1967), 211-212.

Uthoff, G. "The XYY chromosome complement. Brief applications to criminal insanity tests." *St. Louis University Law Journal*, 14(1969), 297-309.

Valentine, G. "The YY chromosome complement." *Clin. Ped.*, 8(1969), 350-355.

Valzelli, L. "Drugs and aggressiveness." *Advances in Pharmacology*, 5(1967), 79-108.

Van Hecke, W. "A case of murder by parathion which nearly escaped detection." *Medicine, Science and the Law*, 4(1964), 197-199.

"Violent prison deaths." *Bulletin of the Canadian Criminology and Corrections Association*, 1(1972).

Vogel-Sprott, M. "Alcohol effects on human behavior under reward and punishment." *Psychopharmacologia*, 11(1967), 337-344.

Vold, G. "Crime in city and county areas." *Annals of the American Academy of Political and Social Science*, 217(1941), 38-45.

———— "Extent and trend of capital crimes in the United States." *Annals of the American Academy of Political and Social Science*, 284(1952), 1-7.

Voss, H., and J. Hepburn. "Patterns in criminal homicide in Chicago." *Journal of Criminal Law, Criminology and Police Science*, 59(1968), 499-508.

Waldo, G. "The criminality level of incarcerated murderers and non-murderers." *Journal of Criminal Law, Criminology and Police Science*, 61(1970), 60-70.

Walker, A. "Murder or epilepsy." *Journal of Nervous and Mental Diseases*, 133 (1961), 430-437.

Walker, H., et al. "Repeated violence." *Criminal Law Review*, 13(1967), 465-472.

Walker, N., et al. "Careers of violence," Oxford University Penal Research Unit, *The Violent Offender—Reality or Illusion?* (Oxford, 1970).

Waller, J. "Accidents and violent behavior: are they related?—Crimes of violence," *Task Force Report on Individual Acts of Violence* (Washington, 1969).

———— "Chronic medical conditions and traffic safety-review of the California experience." *New England Journal of Medicine*, 273(1965), 1413-1420.

Wallerstein, J. "Biological inferiority as a case for delinquency. E. Hooton's findings reviewed and analysed." *Nervous Child*, 6(1947), 467-472.

Walters, R., et al. "Effect of solitary confinement on prisoners." *American Journal of Psychiatry*, 119(1963), 771-773.

Ward, D., et al. "Crimes of violence by women." *Task Force Report on Individual Acts of Violence* (Washington, 1969).

Warder, J. "Two studies of violent offenders." *British Journal of Criminology*, 9 (1969), 389-393.

Wardle, C. "Two generations of broken homes in the genesis of conduct and behaviour disorders in childhood." *British Medical Journal*, 2(1961), 349-354.

Wattenberg, W. "A phenomenon in search of a cause." *Journal of Criminal Law, Criminology and Police Science*, 48(1957), 54-58.

Webb, S. "Crime and division of labor: testing a Durkheimian model." *American*

Journal of Sociology, 78(1972), 643-656.

Weinstein, E. "Symbolic aspects of presidential assassination." *Psychiatry,* 32(1969), 1-11.

Weiss, J. "Suicide. An epidemiologic analysis." *Psychiatric Quarterly,* 28(1954), 226-252.

Weiss, S. "Cry Wolf. A case study of homicide and suicide." *Delaware State Medical Journal,* 35(1963), 293-297.

Weisz, A. "American presidential assassinations." *Diseases of the Nervous System,* 30(1969), 659-668.

Wenk, E., et al. "Can violence be predicted?" *Crime and Delinquency,* 18(1972), 393-402.

Wertham, F. "The cathathymic crisis." *Arch. Neurol. and Psychiatry,* 37(1937), 974.

West, D. "A note on murders in Manhattan." *Medicine, Science and the Law,* 8 (1968), 249-255.

Whittet, M. "The A9 murder." *Criminologist,* 3(1968), 43-65.

Wierner, S. "A normal XYY man." *Lancet* (1968), 1352.

———— "XYY males in a Melbourne prison." *Lancet* (1968), 150.

———— et al. "A murderer with 47 XYY and an additional abnormality." *Australian and New Zealand Journal of Criminology,* 2(1969), 20-28.

Wilbanks, W. "The McKay Commission and the Oswald story: a personal review." *Criminal Law Review,* 9(1972), 124-139.

Wilder, J. "Sugar metabolism in its relation to criminology," Lindauer and Seliger, eds., *Handbook of Correctional Psychology* (New York, 1947).

Wilentz, W. "The alcohol factor in violent deaths." *Am. Pract.,* 12(1961), 829-835.

Williams, A. "The mind of a child murderer." *Mental Health,* 26(1967), 7-8.

———— "The psychopathology of sexual murderers," I. Rosen, ed., *The Pathology and Treatment of Sexual Deviation* (London, 1964).

Williams, D. "Neural factors related to habitual aggression: consideration of differences between those habitual aggressives and others who have committed crimes of violence." *Brain,* 92(1969), 503-520.

Wilmer, H. "Murder, you know." *Psychiatry Quarterly,* 43(1969), 414-447.

Wilson, J., and J. Snodgrass. "The prison code in a therapeutic community." *Journal of Criminal Law, Criminology and Police Science,* 60(1969), 472-478.

Withrop, H. "Creativity in the criminal." *Journal of Social Psychology,* 65(1965), 41-58.

Woddis, G. "Depression and Crime." *British Journal of Delinquency,* 8(1957), 85-94.

Wolfgang, M. "An analysis of homicide-suicide." *Journal of Clinical and Experimental Psychopathology,* 19(1958), 208-218.

———— "Husband and wife homicides." *Journal of Social Therapy,* 2(1956), 263-271.

———— "A preface to violence." *Annals of the American Academy of Political and Social Science,* 364(1966), 1-7.

———— "Quantitative analysis of adjustment to the prison community." *Journal of Criminal Law, Criminology and Police Science,* 51(1961), 607-618.

———— "Social responsibility for violent behavior." *Southern California Law Review,* 43(1970), 5-21.

———— "Socio-economic factors related to crime and punishment in Renaissance

Florence." *Journal of Criminal Law, Criminology and Police Science,* 47(1956), 311-330.

_____ "A sociological analysis of criminal homicide." *Federal Probation,* 25 (1961), 48-55.

_____ "Suicide by means of victim-precipitated homicide." *Journal of Clinical and Experimental Psychopathology,* 20(1959), 335-349.

_____ "Victim compensation in crimes of personal violence." *Minnesota Law Review,* 50(1965), 223-241.

_____ "Victim-precipitated criminal homicide," M. Wolfgang, ed., *Studies in Homicide* (New York, 1967).

_____ "Violence and human behavior," F. Korten et al., eds., *Psychology and the Problems of Society* (Washington, 1970).

_____ "Violence USA: riots and crime." *Crime and Delinquency,* 14(1968), 289-305.

_____ "Who kills whom?" *Psychology Today,* 3(1969), 55-75.

_____ and R. Strohm. "The relationship between alcohol and criminal homicide." *Quarterly Journal of Studies on Alcohol,* 17(1956), 411-425.

_____ et al. "Comparison of the executed and the commuted among admissions to death row." *Journal of Criminal Law, Criminology and Police Science,* 53 (1962), 301-311.

Wood, A. "A socio-structural analysis of murder, suicide and economic crime in Ceylon." *American Sociological Review,* 26(1961), 744-753.

Woods, G. "Crime and heredity." *Australian and New Zealand Journal of Criminology,* 6(1973), 117-118.

Woods, S. "Adolescent violence and homicide: ego disruption and the 6 and 14 dysrhythmia." *Archives of General Psychiatry,* 5(1961), 528-534.

"XYZ chromosome abnormality and criminal behavior." *Connecticut Law Review,* 3(1971), 484-510.

"XYZ chromosome defense." *Georgia Law Journal,* 57(1969), 892-922.

"XYZ error makes men grow tall and go wrong." *Medical World News,* 7(1966), 13.

Zancheck, N. "Homicides and suicides of World War 2. A critical analysis of 656 homicides and 1179 suicides." *Journal of Forensic Science,* 5(1960), 84-101.

Zimmerman, F. "Explosive behavior anomalies in children of an epileptic basis." *New York State Journal of Medicine,* 56(1956), 2537-2543.

Zimring, F. "Is gun control likely to reduce violent killings?" *University of Chicago Law Review,* 35(1968), 721-737.

_____ "The medium is the message. Firearm caliber as a determinant of death from assault." *Journal of Legal Studies,* 1(1972), 97-123.

Zylman, R. "Accidents, alcohol and single cause explanations: lessons from the Grand Rapids study." *Quarterly Journal of Studies on Alcoholism,* Suppl. 4 (1968), 212-233.

Doctoral Dissertations and Other Unpublished Materials

Arnette, J. "The effect of short-term group counseling on anxiety and hostility of newly incarcerated prison inmates." University of Florida, 1967.

Austin, W. "An ethnological analysis of prisoner social structure." University of Georgia, 1972.

Berk, B. "Informal social organization and leadership among inmates in treatment and custodial prisons: a comparative study." University of Michigan, 1962.

Bloom, R. "Effects of tetrahydrocannabinol on aggression in humans." University of Georgia, 1972.

Bramwell, P. "An investigation of the influence of group pressure upon prison inmate leaders and non-leaders." Brigham Young University, 1967.

Brown, V. "Antecedents of aggression, effects of type, intensity and duration." University of California, 1966.

Carter, R. "The federal offender, probationer and prisoner; a descriptive and comparative analysis." University of California at Berkeley, 1966.

Chiswick, N. "Experimental study of the effects of punishment and permission on aggression and aggression anxiety." University of Illinois at Chicago Circle, 1974.

Chuven, H. "Effects of depression, frustration, threat of retaliation and sex of target on physical aggression and anxiety change." University of Alabama, 1973.

Cobb, S. "An exploratory study of episodic violent behavior in selected groups of subjects." University of Alabama, 1973.

Cunningham, R. "Study of the response generalization in aggression among selected personality factors." East Texas State University, 1974.

Curtis, L. "Criminal violence: inquiries into national patterns and behavior." University of Pennsylvania, 1972.

Donnerstein, M. "Threats in the control of aggression." Florida State University, 1973.

Gladdis, R. "The evolution of personality under correctional stress." University of Oregon, 1963.

Galliher, J. "Perceived powerlessness in a hospital and reformatory." Indiana University, 1967.

Geis, G., and J. Monahan. "The social ecology of violence," T. Lickona, ed., *Man and Morality* (New York, in press).

Gordon, A. "Patterns of delinquency in drug addiction." University of London, 1971.

Heffernan, M. "Inmate social systems and subsystems: the 'Square,' the 'Cool' and 'The Life.' " Catholic University of America, 1964.

Humphrey, J. "Homicide, suicide and role relationship in New Hampshire." University of New Hampshire, 1975.

Jaywardene, C. "Criminal homicide: a study in culture conflict." University of Pennsylvania, 1960.

Megargee, E. "Under control and over control in assaultive and homicidal adolescents." University of California at Berkeley, 1964.

Michalowski, R. "Vehicular negligence: the social and criminal patterns of auto traffic fatalities." Ohio State University, 1973.

Moser, R. "Effects of repression, sensitization, arousal, and sex on physical aggression." University of North Dakota, 1972.

Mushanga, M. "Criminal homicide in western Uganda: a sociological study of violent deaths in Ankole, Kigezi and Toro districts of western Uganda." Makerere University, 1970.

O'Keefe, S. "Emotion as a social phenomenon: aggression and status in the classroom." George Peabody College for Teachers, 1973.

Prelesnick, J. "Investigation of the inmate liaison role in the informal communications structure in a maximum security prison psychiatric clinic." Michigan State University, 1972.

Rosenblatt, I. "The effect of punitive measures on attitudes of prison inmates." New York University, 1961.

Rothbart, G. "Social conflict in prison organization." University of Washington, 1964.

Rouse, W. "The problem of adult corrections: a case study of state penal administration in California." Claremont Graduate School, 1962.

Rudoff, A. "Prison inmates: an involuntary association." University of California at Berkeley, 1964.

Schofield, G. "Marijuana: its relation to aggressive behavior." 1968.

Stein, M. "Correlates of aggressiveness in boys in residential treatment." City University of New York, 1974.

Stratton, J. "The measurement of inmate change during imprisonment." University of Illinois, 1964.

White, W. "A factor analytic study of personality characteristics associated with types of criminal violence." U.S. International University, 1974.

Wilson, T. "Some effects of different patterns of management on inmate behavior in a correctional institution." Columbia University, 1965.

Index

125